Philip —

Blessings on your
healing ministry!

Merry Christmas —

Bob G.

BOUNCE

BOUNCE

LIVING THE RESILIENT LIFE

ROBERT J. WICKS

OXFORD
UNIVERSITY PRESS
2010

OXFORD
UNIVERSITY PRESS

Oxford University Press, Inc., publishes works that further
Oxford University's objective of excellence
in research, scholarship, and education.

Oxford New York
Auckland Cape Town Dar es Salaam Hong Kong Karachi
Kuala Lumpur Madrid Melbourne Mexico City Nairobi
New Delhi Shanghai Taipei Toronto

With offices in
Argentina Austria Brazil Chile Czech Republic France Greece
Guatemala Hungary Italy Japan Poland Portugal Singapore
South Korea Switzerland Thailand Turkey Ukraine Vietnam

Copyright © 2010 by Oxford University Press

Published by Oxford University Press, Inc.
198 Madison Avenue, New York, New York 10016
www.oup.com

Oxford is a registered trademark of Oxford University Press

Library of Congress Cataloging-in-Publication Data

Wicks, Robert J. Bounce : living the resilient life / Robert J. Wicks.
p. cm.
Includes bibliographical references and index.
ISBN-13: 978-0-19-536768-3 (cloth : alk. paper)
ISBN-10: 0-19-536768-5 (cloth : alk. paper)
1. Resilience (Personality trait) 2. Positive psychology.
I. Title. BF698.35.R47W54 2010
158.1—dc22   2009006225

Printed in the United States of America on acid-free paper

DEDICATION

Resilience is more than a function of who we are and what we know—as important as both of these factors are. It is also dependent upon those who comprise our personal circle of friends.

In our interpersonal network, it is crucial to have people who believe in us and what we are doing for others—people who consistently stand behind us and provide the resources that allow us to develop and share with others our personal gifts and professional talent.

For me, at this juncture in my life, one of the most significant, quiet voices of generous support and encouragement is Mary Catherine Bunting: retired nurse practitioner, philanthropist, social activist, spiritual model, and friend. And so, it is to Mary Catherine Bunting that I gratefully dedicate this book.

CONTENTS

ACKNOWLEDGMENTS

From its inception, Joan Bossert, vice president and publisher of Oxford University Press was the enthusiastic spirit behind this book. Her belief that a great deal of good might be accomplished by making my writings for helping professionals available to a wider and more general readership was a guiding light for me.

Naturally there are numerous editorial details that must be addressed in preparing a book of this type. Abby Gross, associate editor at Oxford University Press and Anne Livie, my graduate research assistant supported me faithfully in handling so many of them.

As with any major project, there are also persons whose actions and encouragement make all the difference. Included among these certainly must be Judith Needham, Esq., who has served me with her wise counsel and also convinced me of the need for a book like this among lawyers since they frequently interact with persons experiencing great stress, anxiety, loss, and possible physical illness. I do hope this book justifies to some extent her belief in me and what I am doing. Another quiet force of constant support for me and so many others is Joe Molyneaux. He retired from the business world in order to become even more active as a mentor for those in the nonprofit arena. What he does for others is truly an inspiration.

Family support also encourages and sustains the creative energy that underlies the work that I do. My daughter Michaele and son-in-law Peter Kulick never fail to inspire me and my granddaughters Kaitlyn and Emily continue to provide their "Pop-Pop" with unique insights and perspectives that an academic such as I would never achieve on his own.

Finally, my wife Michaele as well as having to edit and re-edit until spots appear before her eyes has helped me improve my work and channel my energies in all the right directions. I may not possess all the talents other writers have but I do have the artistic temperament that accompanies the gift. Through 40 years of married life she has understood, cheered, challenged, and inspired me and for this reason the spirit I have continues to *bounce*.

Thank you one and all.

Robert J. Wicks
Loyola University in Maryland

BOUNCE

Have a Life! An Introduction

*Live all you can; it's a mistake not to. It doesn't so much matter
what you do in particular, so long as you have your life. If you
haven't had that, what have you had?*

HENRY JAMES, *The Ambassadors*

*Periods of stress frequently represent unique opportunities to
develop or strengthen those resilient qualities that are not our
strongest suits.*

FREDERIC FLACH, *Resilience*

Physician and author Walker Percy in one of his novels
poses the question: "What if you missed your life like a
person misses a train?" Unfortunately, in today's stressful world
with multitasking being the norm of the day, this is so easy to
do—especially for those who fail to pay attention to their inner
life and their capacity to grow with experience. Each of us has a
range of resilience (the ability to meet, learn from, and not be
crushed by the challenges and stresses of life). This range is
formed by heredity, early life experiences, current knowledge,
and the level of motivation to meet life's challenges and enjoy
each day to the fullest—no matter what happens! However, of
even more import than the different ranges people have is their
conscious decision to maximize the ways in which they can

3

become as resilient as possible. They may not call this resilience, but it is their ability to be open to life's experience, and so to learn. Those who don't lose an opportunity to enjoy more of life and embrace the challenges thrown their way make the most use of natural pressures and stress which, oddly enough, result in a richer, more meaningful life.

"Having a life" is more than the absence of negative occurrences or pressures. The sources of all stress cannot—and probably should not—be prevented. Yet, they can be limited and, more importantly, as those who study resilience report, the way stress impacts us does not have to be totally negative.

Psychologist Edith Grotberg in her book *Resilience for Today* defines resilience as "the human capacity to deal with, overcome, learn from, or even be transformed by the inevitable adversities of life."[1] What is interesting about this definition is that it points to the unique impact of resilience: If we become the most resilient person we can be, new positive realities and perspectives arise and flourish in the most surprising ways. Amid life's stress and suffering, maybe even *because* of it, when we have the tools to enhance resilience and can strengthen the sense of meaning in our lives, we better appreciate both the welcome and unwelcome aspects of stress.

Each of us has an opportunity to become deeper and more compassionate in response to the stressors in our lives *if* we are aware of some basic practices to contain and understand stress, are mindful, reasonably self-aware, and learn how to maintain a healthy sense of resilience and perspective. In observing and working with physicians, nurses, psychotherapists, educators, relief workers, persons in full-time ministry, and other professional helpers and healers who have demonstrated resilience, I have found that *how* they experience even the most difficult encounters in life is quite telling. So, included in this book are approaches to self-awareness, self-care, compassion, applying positive psychology, self-debriefing, mindfulness, and creating your own resiliency profile that can expand your ability to meet life's challenges in ways similar to those used by healing and helping professionals. This is essential, for as the existentialist writer Albert Camus recognized: "When a person has learned— not merely on paper—how to remain alone with his sufferings, how to overcome his longing to flee, then he has little left to learn."[2]

A physician who was working in Somalia during a devastating famine is a good example of this. During the height of the starvation, he was approached by an interviewer from public radio in the United States with the following question: "Doctor, how can you stand all of this carnage? The old people are dropping like flies. And the children are dying in such numbers that you are stacking them up in the corner like firewood rather than burying them immediately. How can you stand it?" (You could hear the pain in his voice.) The physician stopped, turned to the interviewer and said: "When you watch this horror on television in the United States you are overwhelmed by it, aren't you?" When the reporter nodded, the physician went on. "Well, we in-country feel the same—if not more pain—than all of you, *but* there is one difference." To this, the interviewer (who himself had obviously been in many disaster situations and was quite affected by all of the human tragedy before him) asked in an incredulous voice: "*What* difference?" To which the physician softly responded: "You can't lose hope as long as you are making friends." This may seem like an odd response. Who has time to make friends when people are dying all around you? But this reveals too how personal our responses are to life's stresses. This doctor's response is amazing under the circumstances.

This type of attitude or inner space marked by a sense of resilience, a healthy perspective, and a sense of purpose is not only wonderful for the persons who have it but also is a gift to those who cross their path. *Visvas* is a Sanskrit word that literally translated means "to have trust, to breathe freely, to be without fear." Being able to offer our friends, coworkers, and family the "inner psychological space" of *visvas* can make all the difference both in our own lives and in our personal interactions. Whether we refer to this space as our perspective, attitude, outlook, or the possibly more inclusive term "inner life," it is unique and may often even be countercultural in a society that seems so unnecessarily driven and obsessed by the wrong things.

The "inner or interior life" is what some people point to as a place where nonjudgmental self-awareness, simplicity, freedom, and truth flourish. It is also the psychological or spiritual "place" in which deeply felt healthy needs are experienced and addressed. These include:

A need for permanence in a civilization of transience

A need for silence in the midst of noise

A need for gratitude in the face of unbelievable greed

A need for poverty amid the flaunting of wealth

A need for contemplation [or mindfulness meditation] in a century of action, for without contemplation, action risks becoming mere agitation

A need for communication in a universe content with entertainment and sensationalism

A need for peace amid today's universal outbursts of violence

A need for quality to counterbalance the increasingly prevalent response to quantity

A need for humility to counteract the arrogance of power and science

A need for human warmth when everything is being rationalized or computerized

A need to belong to a small group rather than to be part of the crowd

A need for slowness to compensate for the present eagerness for speed

A need for truth when the real meaning of words is distorted in political speeches and sometimes even in religious discourses

A need for transparency when everything else seems opaque

Yes, a need for *the interior life*.[3]

It is our inner life that includes those psychological factors, belief systems or attitudes, and spiritual or philosophical outlook that provide us with the sources of resilience, a sense of honesty or transparency in our dealings with others. Different psychological approaches, nontheistic philosophies of living (e.g., Buddhism), and world religions all emphasize the need to enhance this sense within us. As we look across the board at these philosophies/psychologies/spiritualities of living, no matter what the approach, they share these themes:

- Recognizing the dangers of psychologically toxic life situations and unhelpful attitudes
- Valuing the need for self-care as an integral part of self-respect
- Having a close, balanced circle of friends
- Knowing the key concepts of resilience that are emphasized by experts in the field
- Appreciating the value of being able to reach out compassionately *without being pulled down*
- Being able to debrief yourself in order to limit stress and improve self-knowledge
- Having the honesty and true humility to see your gifts as clearly as your rough edges
- Discovering and availing yourself of the rich resources of silence, solitude, and mindfulness
- Learning how to develop and reflect upon your own personally developed resilience profile

The approaches in this book represent more than a series of techniques (as important as these may be) for persons who believe that seeking more balance and depth is essential. Instead, these approaches are part of the dramatic process of truly embracing richer a self-knowledge and a more honest self-appreciation. The goal is to live in a compassionate way of giving of ourselves to others, rooted in personal resilience and an ethos that values what is truly good.

And so, becoming more resilient, savoring our brief life, and in turn being able to reach out to others require a serious commitment to go deeper into our own sense of self than even we thought possible. I experienced this personally a number of years ago during one of my regular visits to a personal mentor.

The sessions I had with him were designed to help me keep perspective. At the time (as I am now), I was providing help to other healing and health professionals who were facing their own challenges, darkness, stress, and transitions. As one might expect, helping them to face their own *secondary* stress (the pressures that result in reaching out to others), anxiety, despair and darkness was psychologically dangerous for me as well. My mentor knew this and called on me not to retreat but to begin a journey to understand more deeply my own inner life. I can vividly recall one particular encounter.

We were walking through the Virginia countryside on a crisp, sunny winter day. About halfway through our usual route along the Shenandoah River, he surprised me with the comment: "I think now may be a good time for you to take your inner life more seriously."

Although the statement seemed quite accurate to me at the time, later I wondered why I had not reacted more defensively to it. After all, for almost two years I had been driving an hour and a half each way, every six weeks or so, to see him. I really felt I had been investing good time and energy in being open to the more deeply hidden elements of my inner life that could explain why I did the things I did and reacted as I did. So, my natural response could well have been: "Well, what do you think I have been doing?"

But I think the ideal timing and accuracy of his comment, and the trust I had in him and in our relationship, made me see his words much differently. What I instantly felt he was trying to tell me was that it was time to leap more freely and deeply into what was truly important in life.

I think he meant that I needed to be engaged in a movement toward understanding what made me tick. To ask myself: What drove my work as a caregiver for other caregivers, and what provided a theme and purpose for my personal life? How can I continue to care for others in a professional yet deeply compassionate manner? And how can I truly nurture my own interior life through creative, new, disciplined, and simple ways, to embrace a sense of *resilience* and *mindfulness*?

Upon further reflection, I recognized that to accomplish this, I would need to become even more aware of the very things I had encouraged in others. In other words, I would need to be honest enough to appreciate that when we are not mindful:

- We get upset over too many things
- We look at changes in our lives/our schedules as merely disruptive
- We let quiet compulsions, rhythms, and resistances rule out more and more of living, sapping it of freshness
- We increasingly use the unproductive "once this happens" approach to coping with stress ("Once my children graduate college . . .")
- We increasingly yearn for, and daydream about, having greater simplicity in our lives—without taking any actions to achieve this
- We accept a large disconnect between the healthy way we treat our family, friends, coworkers, and even acquaintances and the manner in which we treat ourselves
- We fail to let our defenses down and instead reject any negative feedback we get rather than trying to really learn, merely becoming chagrined by our errors and personal "growing edges"
- We spend a great deal of our time either in the silver casket of nostalgia or fantasizing about a future when we will be free to do "big things"
- We use our rare quiet moments to ruminate, be resentful, worry, become discouraged, feel lost, bored, or confused instead of finding the renewal that comes from mindfulness practice

- We waste an inordinate amount of time on the trivial—prestige, money, influence, fame, security, and pleasure—while the essential simple joys of life are downplayed or elusive
- We replace passion and commitment with attention only to the mechanics of "doing good" simply out of duty
- We replace a deep respect for patience and pacing one's journey with a need to hurry, achieve, and "finally arrive" (whatever that means)
- We fail to see the moments in our day (waiting in line, a cancellation of an appointment, a brief illness . . .) as spontaneous opportunities for quiet reflection
- We are unable to honor the rhythms of life, and view transitions as annoying or frightening
- We view the ghosts of our past, when they intrude upon our peace and joy, not as teachers who carry valuable information for our growth, but as mere ghosts
- We fall prey to attitudes of arrogance (projection), ignorance (self-condemnation), or discouragement (the need for immediate gratification) rather than being filled with a spirit of *intrigue* about our talents, growing edges, and resistances
- We ignore or belittle our strengths rather than fully prizing them as a pathway to serve others
- We allow our interactions with others to become hackneyed, sprinkled with pat phrases, hollow comments, and worn stories

- We are no longer able to use our love of life to become positively infectious with those we love
- We have few activities in our lives that aren't competitive, for gain, or designed to either add to our sense of security or serve to "medicate" our anxieties and worries
- We have forgotten the major role of courage, the value of simplicity, and the need for transparency in how we lead our lives
- We have sadly lost the desire to be truly sincere and respectful with *ourselves*

But our life doesn't have to be this way. Being aware of these pitfalls, as well as when and where they are especially meaningful for us, can lead to a deeper and more resilient self. Yet, in order to access them, we first need self-awareness, which leads to strength, which leads to an ability to become more resilient—and that is what is at the heart of this brief work.

HOW TO USE THIS BOOK

The essence of this book is concerned with how we know and care for ourselves, so we can cultivate a psychological or spiritual "space" within ourselves that allows us to become resilient and engaged in life—whatever it throws our way. These are interrelated objectives—personal resilience through self-knowledge and self-care on the one hand, and an ability to reach out to embrace experience from a place of inner strength on the other. We explore various approaches to:

- Identifying and reviewing the dangers of denial when we are feeling psychological distress
- Becoming more aware of the ongoing challenges of toxic situations, chronic and acute stress, and unhelpful negative attitudes
- Improving the quality of our self-care protocol or personal renewal program
- Ensuring we have an important balance of friends who challenge, support, tease, and inspire us
- Knowing and internalizing key concepts of resilience
- Seeing the value of compassion (sharing your resilience with others) and knowing how to reach out without being pulled down
- Increasing the awareness of our gifts while becoming more intrigued with, rather than burdened by, our growing edges
- Sensitizing ourselves to the important place of mindfulness and meditation in our daily routine
- Appreciating the joys, nobility, and privilege of being alive in such uncertain times

It is amazing how little it can take to shift the emotional tide in favor of continuously renewing ourselves and strengthening our inner life in today's challenging climate. Even small alterations in behavior can sometimes jumpstart a healthier attitude so we can remain robust and free of undue personal agendas.

In my own life, shortly after graduating from Hahnemann Medical College with my doctorate in psychology, as is common for a young new graduate, I dove into a sea of work. I was teaching full-time at the Graduate School of Social Work and Social Research of Bryn Mawr College, developing and maintaining a psychotherapy caseload of 15 to 20 patients a week, consulting, doing clinical research, writing, and in the process quickly becoming emotionally exhausted myself!

Despite all of this work, I decided to accept "just one more invitation" to speak to a group of educators, on of all topics, "burnout." As I prepared for the talk, I thought, "What a charlatan I am. I'm so fatigued and I am going to address this topic? What a joke!" But an unusual thing happened when I started reading the recent clinical papers and research findings published on burnout. Surprisingly, as I became absorbed by the research on the topic, rather than feeling drained, I slowly but surely began feeling more invigorated by what I read.

Now I could label the problem. I was better able to frame an approach to facing the toxic work stress I was experiencing, and I could improve the overall quality of my personal life as well. In addition, when I brought this awareness—and the increased energy I felt—to the informal self-debriefing I normally undertook at the end of each day (which was a carryover from my early clinical training), I was also able to reinvest myself again in the wonders of my profession. I could recall my original

love for the challenges of clinical psychology rather than mind-
lessly and compulsively moving from task to task. And, I found
myself appreciating and seeking to enhance the major gifts and
talents supervisors had pointed out in me instead of merely
focusing on my shortcomings.

This epiphany that I experienced over 30 years ago has never
totally left me. Instead, it has been reinforced by the new research
and approaches recently published on mindfulness, contemporary positive psychology, and Zen Therapy. It is the source of
the spirit with which I offer this brief book to you.

The following chapters are designed to spur the action necessary to address the question: How can I be more resilient, raise
the quality of my life, and improve the presence I can offer others as a result of these actions? Not to expend the energy to
address this question in today's stressful and insecure world is,
at the most basic level, impractical and unfair both to us and to
those who need us in their lives.

RECOGNIZING AND DEALING
WITH DENIAL

Given the delicate nature of our interactions with family, friends,
and fellow workers, if we avoid employing the simple, powerful
principles that allow us to increase resilience and limit stress, we
hazard emotionally and physically burning out. And yet, many
of us still opt to do this at times. Two noted experts on the

human psyche, Jeffrey Kottler and Richard Hazler, observe rationalizations that allow us to avoid facing our own challenges and increasing the strength of our inner life. All of us are familiar with these following rationalizations:

- "This period will pass. I am just busier right now."
- "I have a lot of experience and know how to keep the stress that I am experiencing in my private life out of my work."
- "None of my colleagues or family has complained to me about my not being effective or dependable, so I am still really okay."
- "I am a person with great skills, so I can deal with this difficulty without any input from others."

If there is an apt proverb for the articulated and unspoken demands people make of us in today's often crazy world, it surely must be the Yiddish one: "Sleep faster . . . We need the pillows!" In addition to the unrealistic expectations we face, the stakes are now extremely high for those of us who want to live a rich and full life while still dealing effectively with stressful family and work situations. As a result, the potential for our developing such psychological problems as emotional blunting at one end of the spectrum or extreme emotionality on the other are quite great. Yet, many of us still deny our own personal emotional needs—possibly as a misguided survival mechanism of some sort.

It is no surprise then that we can become so discouraged at times because we don't even know there are practical approaches that not only deal with environmental and personal sources of stress, but can also raise the quality of life at work and at home. Instead, unfortunately, we just march on because we have no other realistic choice.

I encountered this attitude during a session with one very competent counselor who was starting to manifest early symptoms of chronic secondary stress—things like hypersensitivity, increased daily use of alcohol, and sleep disturbance. When I asked him how he would characterize his own problem, he said, "I may not be burned out yet." Then, after a brief pause, he smiled slightly and added, "But I think I'm experiencing at least a brownout!"

Acknowledging his insight into his precarious situation, I asked what type of personal renewal program (what professionals sometimes refer to as a "self-care protocol") he hoped to design and employ for himself to prevent further deterioration of his emotional well-being. In response, after sighing, he said, "I only wish I had the time for something like that!"

Time, of course, is limited for all of us today. More and more I am aware of this even in my own life. Shortly, after I received my doctorate, a physician who had one of the busiest practices in the area came in for an initial psychological assessment. He was having an extramarital affair. Being a new graduate, I remember carefully formulating a complex Freudian theoretical diagnosis in my mind. If he were to come in to see me now, I must confess that my first unspoken reaction would be: "Where does he find the time?"

While we need to schedule our priorities and ensure that what we do is accomplished in the most effective way possible, no matter how tumultuous our lives are, we must take care of our own needs as well. If we don't want to burn out completely, we need to make certain activities part of our daily routine.

Persons in the medical and nursing professions realize that "for every poisoned worker there are a dozen with subclinical toxicity."[4] "Subclinical" simply means these individuals don't yet meet the criteria for the disorder but they are close. So, for every person experiencing serious psychological impairment in our interpersonal network, there are at least another dozen or so of us who are starting to manifest some of the symptoms of chronic or acute stress—but may not even realize it until well after the fact. Given this, the only sound approach is to be proactive in addressing not just the dangers underlying our daily routines, but the ways that those very challenges can be channeled to help us strengthen our inner reserves—*because of*, not simply in spite of, these challenges.

Ignoring the sources and effects of stress in our life is one of the most insidious dangers to our sense of well-being. Fortunately, such an unproductive style practically atrophies of its own accord once we accept the following simple reality:

> The seeds of daily and serious stress and the seeds of true passionate involvement in life are actually the *same* seeds

Once again, the question is *not* whether stress will appear in our lives. Instead, the real beneficial question is: To what extent will we take essential steps to appreciate, limit, and learn from chronic and traumatic stress in order to deepen our inner lives and to remain productive and creative?

Each of us faces many pressures, not only in the work arena but also in our personal lives. A difficult marriage, raising adolescents, physical illness, financial pressures, and loss of loved ones—sometimes the list seems endless. But these problems are often exacerbated by the unrealistic time and energy we dedicate to finding solutions to these problems. A good illustration of this is that in most work settings today, stress prevention courses are offered. However, when a list of the problems we must face is presented and reviewed, the oft heard "back of the room" response by those attending is: "Yes, I knew that all along. So what? There's nothing you can do about it. It's part of the territory." Then, when a long list of stress reducers is subsequently offered by the presenter, unconsciously the response to that may also be to put these recommendations in a "mental drawer" marked: "Nice if I had the time or energy, but totally unrealistic given the myriad demands of my schedule." And to some extent this may well be true. In all honesty, who has the time for half of what is suggested in these workshops or in the many books on stress prevention? (As a matter of fact, even pondering some of the recommended stress reduction steps may become in itself stressful!) On the other hand, we don't have much choice. If we resist self-knowledge and self-care, we will never take control of stress in our lives.

The premise of this book is tied to a significantly different question than the one posed above. It is not: Who has the time to follow a long list of suggestions? Instead, it is: Who in their right mind would not take out the time to ponder the *essentials* of self-knowledge, self-care, and resilience?

The practical steps for maintaining self-care and achieving a new perspective are actually quite simple. Yet, what is also true and must be admitted is that these steps are not always easy to undertake because of well-entrenched habits and our current workloads (which include the reality of multitasking both at home and work). These logjams of resistance can be dealt with by taking incremental steps and following the guidelines for self-care and personal debriefing presented in this book—and then *acting upon any insights gained in some small initial way.* That is neither impossible nor unrealistic.

Psychologists Karen Reivich and Andrew Shatte say in their book, *The Resilience Factor*:

> Everyone needs resilience. More than fifty years of scientific research have powerfully demonstrated that resilience is the key to success at work and satisfaction in life. Where you fall on the resilience curve—your natural reserves of resilience— affects your performance in school and at work, your physical health, your mental health, and the quality of your relation- ships. It is the basic ingredient to happiness and success.[5]

So given this, the goal of *Bounce* is to provide practical approaches to enhance the essential ingredient of resilience and, in the process, raise the quality of our lives. These are crucial goals for all of us—especially in today's challenging times.

NOTES

1. Grotberg, E. (2003). *Resilience for today: Gaining strength from adversity.* Westport, CT: Praeger Publishers.

2. Camus, A. Source unknown.

3. Dubois, D. (1983). Renewal of prayer. *Lumen Vitae,* 38(3), 273–274.

4. Scott, C., & Hawk, J. (Eds.). (1986). *Heal thyself: the health of health care professionals.* New York: Brunner/Mazel Publishers, Inc.

5. Reivich, K., & Shatte, A. (2002). *The resilience factor: Seven keys to finding your inner strength and overcoming life's hurdles.* New York: Broadway Books.

Navigating Life's Rough Waters: Riding the Crest of Chronic and Acute Stress

We have the human capacity to become resilient, which allows us to deal with the bombardment of events causing so much stress. And in dealing with these events we become stronger, more confident in our abilities, more sensitive to the stress others are experiencing and even more able to bring about change to minimize or eradicate the sources of stress . . . We are not implying that resilience protects us from these stresses, these risks, these dangers. That is not the role of resilience. We want protections, yes, but resilience involves not only supports, strengths, and skills, but actions to deal with the inevitable adversities we all face in life.

EDITH GROTBERG, *Resilience for Today*

There is no getting around all the stresses associated with day-to-day living. In many cases, it is just not possible to remove them. Instead, facing them productively is like tacking through rough waters. In his book *First You Have to Row a Little Boat*, former advertising executive Richard Bode describes this approach quite well:

To tack a boat, to sail a zigzag course, is not to deny our destination or our destiny—despite how it may appear to those who never dare to take the tiller in their hand. Just the opposite: It's to recognize the obstacles that stand between ourselves and where we want to go, and then to maneuver with patience and fortitude, making the most of each leg of our journey, until we reach our landfall.[1]

To my mind, "tacking" is an ideal metaphor for the way we often must plot our personal journey. To ignore what must be faced or simply seek to take everything head-on may be disastrous both personally and professionally. On the other hand, knowledge and maturity help us to psychologically tack the stressful waters that we sometimes encounter so that we can make the most of all that we face in our personal lives and at work. Such navigation must include a basic appreciation of the elements of both chronic and acute stress.

CHRONIC STRESS

Each day we deal with stress. We may be running late, dealing with minor complaints, arguing with a friend, having problems with an adolescent in the family, dealing with a parent who needs nursing home care, have a coworker who is dragging his feet on a project, or perhaps we are not feeling well physically or did not receive the positive job evaluation we expected. In the aggregate, these common, daily pressures represent what we term "chronic stress." While in themselves such problems are not major ones, over a period of time they can sap us of energy. If left unchecked or inappropriately dealt with they can lead to serious burnout of our energy and may require professional intervention and support. Knowing this, Russian playwright Anton Chekhov—in the colorful ways he is known for—once proclaimed: "Any idiot can face a crisis—it's this day-to-day living that wears you out."[2]

The problem for many of us is that the causes of burnout are often so quiet and insidious that we fail to notice them until they have caused great harm. The psychiatrist in the novel *The Case of Lucy Bending* laments the way burnout creeps up on you undetected:

> Most laymen, he supposed, believed psychiatrists fell apart under the weight of other people's problems. Dr. Theodore Levin had another theory. He feared that a psychiatrist's life force gradually leaked out. It was expended on sympathy, understanding, and the obsessive need to heal and help create whole lives. Other people's lives. But always from the outside. Always the observer. Then one day he would wake up and discover that he himself was empty, drained.[3]

Communication theorist Marshall McLuhan put it another way: "If the temperature of the bath rises one degree every ten minutes, how will the bather know when to scream?"[4] Today, family demands, financial pressures, multitasking, and a psychologically toxic work environment are but a few of the pressures we must face that collectively cause chronic stress.

TOXIC WORK

In her book, *Toxic Work*, Barbara Bailey Reinhold notes:

> The syndrome of toxic work overtakes you when what's hap-
> pening to you at work causes protracted bouts of distress,
> culminating in emotional suffering or physical symptoms and
> heightened by the perceived inability to stop the pain and
> move on to find or create a more rewarding situation. Feeling
> stuck where you are, unable to imagine or take your next
> steps, is perhaps the most debilitating part of the problem.[5]

So, quite simply, a toxic work environment is one in which we
can no longer productively work. Our creative powers are
thwarted and our natural resources are drained. And this level
of psychological "toxicity" in the workplace is not going to get
better in the near future. We should expect more of the same.
Not a day goes by that we don't hear about our failing economy
and a looming recession, layoffs, cost-cutting, rising oil prices,
global warming, a protracted war abroad, a housing and mort-
gage crisis, and the list goes on.

Being nostalgic for the "good old days," while understandable, will not carry us today. Reinhold offers an example from
nursing that can well apply to persons serving in any number of
professions and occupations:

> Marjorie, a nurse in the day-surgery unit, told me, "We
> can't wait for this time of cost-cutting to be over, so we can

go back to practicing the way we were trained." . . . She belonged to a cadre of "good old days" complainers who gathered in the hospital snack bar at break time each morning . . .

Fortunately, Marjorie had a friend in pediatrics who had stopped going to the "bitch and moan" sessions, as she called them, because she believed they made things worse . . . "These are the new policies, and they're not going away," she told Marjorie, "so why don't we go to the hospital fitness room together tomorrow and ride the stationary bikes instead?" Marjorie tried it, was shocked at how different it made her feel.[6]

We can see the essence of a toxic culture at work in this hospital—a setting in which workers have a difficult time letting go of the past and get stuck. Action is not taken to break the "bitch and moan" routine. In the next chapter, a self-care program is presented that includes actions to stave off the dangers of chronic and acute stress. But before we can act, we need to become aware of the signs of burnout.

DEFINITION AND CAUSES OF BURNOUT

Psychologist Herbert Freudenberger, who coined the term "burnout," described it as "a depletion or exhaustion of a person's mental and physical resources attributed to his or her prolonged, yet unsuccessful striving toward unrealistic expectations, internally or externally derived."[7]

Since Freudenberger introduced this term, the need for a unique concept of burnout has been questioned since the same symptoms and signs are seen in other disorders like depression and anxiety. So, when referring to burnout and the interventions needed to prevent or limit it, some professionals feel it is confusing the issue unnecessarily. But many in the field—including myself—feel that the term is still quite helpful. If nothing else, the term "burnout" implicitly recognizes it is "legitimate" for persons to be distressed when experiencing life's daily stresses, anxiety, and disappointments. The causes for burnout are legion, so trying to pin down one source of burnout is futile.

Most researchers and authors on the topic of burnout (including me) have developed their own tailored list of the causes of burnout. (Take a look at Table 1 if you need help in thinking about causes.)

Underlying all of the causes of burnout is a perception of something *lacking*, which produces frustration and hinders us from taking action. It can be a lack of education, opportunity, free time, ability, the chance to ventilate, institutional power, variety, meaningful tasks, criteria to measure impact, coping mechanisms, staff harmony, professional and personal recognition, insight into one's motivations, and balance in one's schedule. Since these factors are present to some degree in all our lives, the potential for burnout is always present.

Table I   Causes for Burnout

- Inadequate quiet time, physical rest, cultural diversion, education, and personal psychological replenishment
- Vague criteria for success or inadequate positive feedback on efforts made
- Guilt over failures, and over taking out time to nurture oneself properly to deal with one's own legitimate needs
- Unrealistic ideals that are threatening rather than motivating
- Inability to deal with anger or other interpersonal tensions
- Extreme need to be liked by others, prompting unrealistic involvement with others
- Poor community life or unrealistic expectations and needs surrounding the support and love of others for us
- Working with people (peers, superiors, those coming for help) who are burned out
- Extreme powerlessness to effect needed change or being overwhelmed by paperwork and administrative tasks
- A serious lack of appreciation by our superiors, colleagues, or those whom we are trying to serve
- Sexism, ageism, racism, or other prejudice experienced directly in our lives and work
- High incidence of conflict in the family, home, work, or living environment
- A serious lack of charity and respect among those with whom we must live or work
- Extreme change during times in life when maturational crises and adjustments are also occurring (for example, a 48-year old physician who is being asked to work with patients diagnosed with cancer at a time when she has just been diagnosed with cancer herself)
- Seeing money wasted on projects that seem to have no relation to helping people
- Not having the freedom or power to deal with or remove oneself from regularly occurring stressful events
- The "savior complex"—an inability to recognize what we can and cannot do
- Overstimulation or isolation and alienation

Consequently, every person truly engaged with their work is in danger of impairment in some way to some extent. Unfortunately though, care is usually only sought and provided when a person is seriously enough impaired to require professional help. It is also very difficult for many people to admit their difficulties unless they have reached crisis proportions— and even then some still deny problems. As W. H. Auden aptly noted, "Conscious insensitivity is a self-contradiction."[8]

And so, even though the topic of chronic stress is not a new or novel one, the danger of burnout still exists as a serious threat to our psychological welfare, making greater awareness of the symptoms, signs, and causes of burnout quite necessary for those interested in enhancing resilience in their lives. We can detect the signs of burnout in all of the following statements made by persons who feel they must simply endure:

- *Cynicism*: "I just see this as a job. Being in my field of work is not what it used to be. Nothing is going to change. People ask me such trivial questions and burden me with stupid things."
- *Workaholism*: "I need to constantly check my e-mail and voice mail even when I am not working on the weekend." "My husband and I need to earn a down payment for a house so I have to work more shifts than I'd like."
- *Isolation*: "I really don't feel part of things on the job. The other employees are nice people, but I feel so different and isolated from them. I never discuss my work or personal life with any of them."

- *Boredom*: "I am so tired of doing the same thing every day. When I'm not killing myself, I'm bored to tears. If I hadn't invested so much in this field already, I would get out. I can't wait until the end of a shift or the workday."
- *Depletion*: "I feel it is taking me longer and longer to do less and less. I no longer feel the passion about the job as I did in the past. I am tired before I begin. I don't quite dread going into work, but it certainly is getting to that point. All I think about is the job."
- *Conflict*: "Everything seems to get on my nerves now. I fight with the persons I am paid to serve, am irritable with colleagues, and am no fun to be with at home. I also resent that people are asking too much from me."
- *Arrogance*: "I wish I didn't have to deal with such incompetent coworkers. Also, I wish persons at work and in my family would just follow what I tell them to do."
- *Helplessness:* "I am not sure I really can do anything to change my situation. This is the workload I have to deal with, plain and simple. Also, my sleeping is often disturbed, I have no time for family and friends, my sinuses are always bothering me, and I know I drink too much coffee in the morning and too much wine in the evening."

But simply *avoiding* the dangers of burnout (as important as this may be) may not be enough. We should also take clear steps to *prevent* the acceleration of the stresses already prevalent in our work and home life. To do this, it is important to appreciate the levels of burnout and to take out time to identify potential problem areas and review how they are being addressed. (Developing a self-tailored Personal Vulnerability Profile is a key resource for avoiding the hazards of insidious burnout and is provided later in this chapter for your use.)

LEVELS OF BURNOUT

The symptoms of chronic stress include frustration, depression, apathy, helplessness, impatience, disengagement, emotional depletion, cynicism, hopelessness, a significant decline in one's professional self-esteem and confidence, feeling overwhelmed, and anhedonia (being unable to experience pleasure). For our purposes here, it may be helpful to break down how burnout progresses for illustrative purposes, even though there is significant overlap between the levels of burnout.

Psychiatrist James Gill provides a particularly helpful discussion of how burnout progresses:

> The *first level* [see Table 2] is characterized by signs and symptoms that are relatively mild, short in duration and occur only occasionally . . . The *second level* [see Table 4] is reached when signs and symptoms have become *more stable, last longer* and are *tougher* to get rid of . . . The *third level* is experienced when signs and symptoms have become *chronic* and a *physical illness* has developed."[9]

This commonsense breakdown describes the progression of burnout to the point where self-administered measures have

Table 2   Level 1. Daily Burnout: A Sampling of Key Signs and Symptoms

- Mentally fatigued at the end of the day
- Feeling unappreciated, frustrated, bored, tense, or angry as a result of contact(s) with family, colleagues, supervisors, superiors, assistants, or others
- Experiencing physical symptoms (headache, backache, upset stomach, etc.)
- Pace of day's activities or requirements of present tasks seem greater than personal or professional resources available
- Tasks required on the job are repetitious, beyond our ability, or require intensity on a continuous basis

failed, and psychological and medical assistance is now necessary. This may mean entering or reentering psychotherapy and obtaining medical help. Once the threshold of the third level has been crossed, the burnout is severe and remediation of the problem will likely take a good deal of time and effort. This is why preventive measures are essential.

As I've already pointed out, the seeds of burnout and the seeds of enthusiasm are in reality the same seeds. The commitment to others and to our work that fuels our enthusiasm can be the same energy that causes us to ignore our own needs and inadvertently depletes our inner resources. And so, anyone who truly cares can expect that they will need to ride the waves of burnout—and occasionally get knocked down by a wave they missed! Basic steps in averting burnout (see Table 3) should, in most cases, prevent many of these difficulties.

Table 3   Level 1. Daily Burnout: Steps for Dealing with "Daily Burnout"

- Correcting errors in thinking so there is greater recognition of when we are exaggerating or personalizing situations in an inappropriate or negative way
- Having a variety of activities in one's daily schedule
- Getting sufficient rest
- Faithfully incorporating meditation (or quiet reflective time) into our daily schedule
- Interacting on a regular basis with supportive friends
- Being assertive
- Getting proper nourishment and exercise

It may be difficult to detect when level 1 inches toward level 2, but for our purposes, what is important is being self-aware. Problems have escalated and symptoms have gradually become intractable to brief interventions. Now, a more profound effort is necessary (see Table 4). Central to such action is a willingness to reorient priorities and take risks with our style of dealing with the world, which for some reason is not working optimally. To accomplish this, frequently our mentor and colleagues need to become involved. Their support and insight for dealing with the distress are needed. The uncomfortable steps taken to unlock ourselves from social problems and the temptation to deal with them in a single unproductive way—such as working after hours every day even when our health is starting to fail and the quality of our work is beginning to suffer dramatically—require all of the guidance and support we can obtain. In many cases, a vacation or retreat is necessary in order to distance

Table 4   Level 2. Minor Stress becomes Distress: Major Signs and Symptoms

- Idealism and enthusiasm about being in one's occupation or profession is waning; disillusionment about work begins surfacing on a regular basis
- Experiencing a general loss of interest in yourself for a period of a month or longer
- Pervasive feelings of boredom, stagnation, apathy, and frustration
- Being ruled by schedule; no longer being attuned to people or customers we work with; viewing them impersonally and without thought
- Losing criteria with which to judge the effectiveness of work
- Inability to get refreshed by the other elements in one's life, such as a good book or movie
- A loss of interest in professional resources—breakthroughs in the field, books, conferences, innovations
- Intermittent but lengthy (lasting a week or more) periods of irritation, depression, and stress which do not seem to lift even with some effort to correct the apparent causes

ourselves from the demands of work so that revitalization and reorientation can occur.

All of us sometimes experience level 1 burnout as part of the ups and downs of living fully in a stressful world. Most involved individuals also experience level 2 burnout at times. And some unfortunately move to level 3. This is why self-awareness and self-knowledge are essential. Beyond this, if we face stress constructively, not only do we mitigate its toxicity, but we also are in a position to learn from it in a way that girds us. But this requires both the right type of knowledge and the humility to

turn to others for help when we don't progress as we should—
not an easy task when people often assume that because we are
intelligent, healthy adults, we are always strong, always there,
and naturally, always right. The reality, however, is far removed
from the perceptions that family members, colleagues, and
coworkers may impose on us. We are all personalities-in-
process. We have growing edges and are vulnerable to particular
stresses, situations, and colleagues. As a result, it would help
immeasurably for us to be aware, through self-questioning, of
where these vulnerable points are so we are not caught unawares.

PERSONAL VULNERABILITY PROFILE

All of us are psychologically vulnerable at times. No matter how
healthy and experienced we are, being aware of the situations,
problems, and people that are most likely to trigger stress in us
is the first step to a healthy response.

Take a moment to consider the questions in Table 5.

By addressing questions like these honestly and completely,
we can begin to see the areas where we have progressed and
developed effective coping skills. Other areas may need attention—sometimes *constant* attention—given our ingrained personality style. To ignore these areas is to court unnecessary
stress. As a matter of fact, even when we ourselves don't feel the
stress, this can translate into a problem. As one professional
told me when I questioned him about his problems with stress,

Table 5   Personal Vulnerability Profile

- How do you deal with persons who are very demanding?
- How do you blunt ("medicate") the pain you experience in your work and family life?
- In what instances do you "dump" on coworkers or family?
- What type of person "gets to you"?
- How do you handle the unrealistic expectations of your job?
- What past personal and professional failures haunt you, and how have you learned from them?
- What prevents you from fully responding to life at home and in the work setting?
- How do you handle unscheduled events in the day?
- What are the things that you tend to lie to yourself about or hide from coworkers and family?
- What triggers your anger most easily?
- What do you feel you are most insecure about?
- What is having the greatest negative impact on both your professional and personal lives?
- How have you addressed the imbalances in your home life (with spouse, children, and friends) given the intensity of work?
- What are the ways you address problems at work such as understaffing or poorly trained staff, incompetence or poor work ethics, chronic complaining, rigidity, narrow compartmentalizing of responsibilities and not stepping beyond these roles, and overcompensation by some to deal with weaknesses of others?
- When do you find yourself not listening to family or friends because you feel emotionally exhausted or see their problems as less important than those of people at work?
- What themes run through your daydreams and night dreams?
- What recent events at home and work produce in you the most guilt, resentment, or embarrassment?
- When are you the most bored with work and what do you do about it?
- What are the coping mechanisms you use when you feel overwhelmed?

"I don't think I really am usually under stress, but I think I'm a carrier!" When we do induce stress in others, we in turn can make life difficult for fellow workers or family members, and this creates burnout contagion which will eventually come back to haunt us, the "carriers." That is why it is good to have some familiarity with the approaches necessary to lessen the stress in those around us even if we may not be experiencing it ourselves.

ACUTE STRESS

Overwhelming stress when its onset is sudden and dangerous to our psychological and physical health is referred to as "acute." Psychologist Jeffrey Kottler had this to say about the threats to his personal sense of well-being that were a by-product of his work as a therapist: "Never mind that we catch our clients' colds and flus, what about their pessimism, negativity . . . Words creep back to haunt us. Those silent screams remain deafening."[10] What he is obviously speaking about here is the destabilization of our own personality when we come in contact with the severe psychological, physical, and sexual trauma experienced by others around us.

Given the trauma many people have to deal with in today's violent world, along with daily chronic stress, acute stress is an ever-present danger. Increasingly all of us are called upon to ease the suffering of our family, coworkers, and even new acquaintances who are experiencing psychic trauma. When this mixes with the acute stress we may experience in our own lives— including marital, financial, personal, and world instability— the result may be quite psychologically toxic. This unrecognized or unaccepted emotional state can lead to severe impairment or a psychological "grayness" in how we experience our life, as well as disturbed interpersonal relationships with those close to us.

One of the most sensible approaches to recognizing, limiting, avoiding, and even learning from the onset of acute stress is to conduct daily debriefings with yourself. A second approach is to have an organized way to question yourself to uncover the presence or duration of signs and symptoms of possible post-traumatic stress disorder (PTSD)—which represents the cluster of reactions that we might encounter in ourselves following a traumatic experience (rape, abuse, terrorism, school shooting, serious automobile accident, natural disaster, armed robbery). These two approaches go hand in hand.

In doing this we can learn from the experiences of persons in the helping professions when they at times lose distance and are temporarily swept away by the expectations, needs, painful experiences, and negativity of others. They are educated to pick up these signs as early as possible so they are not unnecessarily dragged down. We can learn much from how they avoid losing perspective or regain it when they temporarily lose their way. The emotional distance from tragedy that professional helpers cultivate and value is a good approach for us to use when we must deal with the pain of others.

The Russian proverb comes to mind: "When you live next to the cemetery, you can't cry for everyone who dies." Most of us, whether we are professional helpers or not, too often tend to absorb the sadness, anxiety, and negativity of those around us. Sometimes we even feel this is expected of us. As we listen to or observe stories of terrible things that happen to others, we "catch" some of their futility, fear, vulnerability, and hopelessness rather than experiencing mere frustration or concern. We learn that no matter how prepared we are, we are not immune to the psychological and spiritual dangers that arise in living a full life of involvement with others.

I remember learning this the hard way myself. In 1994 I did a psychological debriefing of some of the relief workers evacuated from Rwanda's bloody civil war. I interviewed each person and gave them an opportunity to tell their stories. As they related the horrors they had experienced, they seemed to be grateful for an opportunity to vent. They recounted the details again and again, relating their feelings as well as descriptions of the events which triggered them. Their sense of futility, their feelings of guilt, their sense of alienation, their experiences with emotional outbursts, all came to the fore.

In addition to listening, I gave them handouts identifying experiences they might have down the road (problems sleeping, difficulties trusting and relating to others, flashbacks, and the like). As I moved through the process of debriefing and providing information so they could have a frame of reference for understanding their experiences, I thought to myself, "This is going pretty well." Then, something happened that shifted my whole response.

In the course of one of the final interviews, a relief worker related stories of how certain members of the Hutu tribe raped and dismembered their Tutsi foes. Soon, I noticed I was holding onto my chair for dear life. I was doing what some young people call "white-knuckling it."

After the session, I did what I usually do after an intense encounter—a thorough review of my feelings, cognitions (ways of thinking, perceiving, and understanding an event and my reactions to it), and beliefs. If time doesn't permit a break then, I do it at the end of the day—every day. In doing this, I get in touch with my feelings by asking myself: What made me sad? Overwhelmed me? Sexually aroused me? Made me extremely happy or even confused me? Being brutally honest with myself, I try to put my finger on the pulse of my emotions. The first thing that struck me about this particular session was the tight grip I had on the chair as the session with the relief worker progressed. "What was I feeling when I did this? Why did I do this?"

It didn't take me long to realize that their terrible stories had broken through my defenses and normal sense of distance and detachment. I was holding onto the chair because, quite simply, I was frightened to death that if I didn't I would be pulled into the vortex of darkness myself.

That recognition alone helped lessen the pain and my fearful uneasiness. I then proceeded with a personal debriefing to prevent another slide into the vortex and to learn—and thus benefit—from the events of the day.

A few fairly straightforward questions in such a debriefing can help us to determine whether a problem is present due to a traumatic encounter. We can also encounter problems when interacting with someone close to us who has experienced trauma as in the case of a parent listening to the story of her child's experience of sexual abuse or a spouse's experiences in a war zone (see Table 6).

The essential frame of reference to use in understanding this self-questioning is that having these symptoms is no more a sign of personal weakness than having the symptoms of any psychological or medical disorder. This is important to note at the outset so that neither self-blame, self-debasement, nor bravado prevent a careful self-examination—especially after a particularly difficult encounter. Interacting over a period of time with persons experiencing sexual, physical, or emotional violence would take a toll on anyone.

To ensure that persons consider these perils when they take time out for self-reflection, I point them to the following general principles to keep in mind when seeking self-understanding following traumatic encounters:

- Be as nonjudgmental and accepting of yourself as you would be in dealing with others who have undergone a traumatic event
- Constantly remember that the symptoms you are experiencing as a result of the traumatic encounter(s) are related to

Table 6 Questions to Ask Yourself to Uncover Vicarious PTSD

If one or more of the following symptoms/signs have lasted longer than one month and are presently interfering with your personal and work life, care must be taken to consider that the result of being constantly exposed to persons who have experienced trauma may be having a vicarious impact on you:

1. Do you find that you are reexperiencing past personal traumatic events or ones shared by others in your life? Are you experiencing:
   - Nightmares?
   - Intrusive thoughts about persons in your interpersonal network who have experienced trauma?
   - Flashbacks to stories that family members or people at work have shared, or to your own traumatic experience?
   - The reliving of trauma or interactions with others in your life who have experienced trauma?
   - The association of events in the present with past personal trauma or the traumatic experiences of others?

2. Are you experiencing a blunting of affect, numbing, loss of feelings, or tendency to avoid reminders of a past traumatic event?
   - Feeling a sense of detachment or restriction in the range of emotions you feel?
   - Avoiding thoughts, feelings, conversations, people, or activities that are reminders of past traumatic content related by others?
   - Having memory lapses with respect to past trauma-laden events?
   - Having a morbid view of the future?

3. Do you have a heightened/exaggerated sense of arousal?
   - Hyperalert or usually feeling "on guard"?
   - Pronounced startle reaction?
   - Irritability or a "short emotional fuse" with colleagues, family, and acquaintances?
   - Problems concentrating, sleeping, eating, or enjoying normal activities that previously brought you pleasure or provided a sense of mastery?

(continued)

Table 6 Continued

4. Do you experience dramatic alterations in your outlook or worldview?
   • Personal sense of safety/trust is fragile?
   • Positive view of the human condition is absent or overshadowed by a jaded sense of life?
   • View of one's own efficacy and personal self-confidence is now questioned?
   • Awareness of cruelty or fragility of life (given your own trauma or that of others) is often present in a depressing, somewhat frightening way?
   • Feelings of shame, guilt, depression, or worthlessness are present more and more?
5. Have you begun to demonstrate symptoms/exaggerated signs of antisocial or asocial behavior not present prior to the overwhelming/ongoing exposure to anothers' trauma or your own?
   • Dangerous behavior (i.e. sexual promiscuity, erratic/aggressive/careless driving patterns, fiscal irresponsibility, poor work habits, etc.)?
   • Extreme irresponsibility in one's personal and professional lives?
   • Alcohol abuse, illegal drug use, self-medication, criminal behavior?
6. Are your basic interpersonal relations becoming dramatically affected?
   • Suspicious, cynical, or hypercritical style is now present?
   • Boundary violations with patients, colleagues, and friends are present?
   • Loss of interest in activities at home or work?
   • Poor patterns of self-care resulting in alterations in interactions with others?
   • Lack of availability at work and to family and friends?

the experience(s) themselves rather than to some inherent personality weakness or lack of personality strength in yourself

• Know that when you are dealing with trauma over a period of time, rather than as a single event, that dealing with the symptoms and dangers of vicarious PTSD on an ongoing basis is to be expected

• Share your feelings and concerns with others—it is psychologically wise to do so and those who seek to go it alone either wind up drawing back from being compassionate or acting out in unhealthy ways (alcoholism, over-detachment, promiscuity, etc.)

Although we hear a lot about PTSD today—especially after the September 11th attacks—it is far from a new phenomenon. Given this, the following succinct summary is offered as a brief review before moving on to the next chapter, where we look at helpful ways we can care for ourselves and build resilience.

Surviving a life-threatening personal experience often produces intense psychological reactions in the forms of intrusive thoughts about the experience and fear-related avoidance of reminders. In the first few weeks following a traumatic experience these patterns are found in most individuals and thus seem to represent a natural response mechanism for psychological adaptation to a life-changing event. Persistence of this reaction pattern at troublesome levels beyond a three-month period, however, indicates that the natural psychological adjustment process, like mourning in the bereaved, has been derailed. At that point the psychological reactions natural in the first few weeks become symptoms of PTSD. In other words, PTSD may be seen as the persistence of a natural process beyond its natural time frame for resolutions.

The cardinal features of PTSD are trauma-specific symptoms of intrusion, avoidance, and physical arousal. The primary requirement is the presence of . . . A life-threatening event, such as serious injury in a traffic accident, would satisfy this criterion, while the expected death of a loved one from natural causes would not.[11]

There are classic signs of PTSD that include intrusive thoughts about the trauma, recurring nightmares, and flashbacks. As these symptoms persist, many individuals begin to cope by avoiding encounters and places that remind them of the trauma. They in essence begin to withdraw from life. They may experience numbing on the one hand or become hypervigilant on the other.

It's understandable how these symptoms take hold if we consider these as survival responses, built into our psychology by years of evolution. After a trauma we have learned that a particular setting may be life threatening. War is life threatening! The problem is when these reactions are generalized to everyday encounters and perceptions. For the veterans returning from war, a car backfiring sounds a lot like gunfire, and they react accordingly.

Recognizing the signs of PTSD is essential so that professional help can be sought before unhealthy patterns of behavior take hold. When PTSD disrupts our frame of reference, the results may change our worldview, sense of professional and personal identity, and spiritual, psychological, or philosophical outlook. The negative ripple effect may lead to personal alienation from friends, coworkers, and even the relationship we have with ourselves. It can cause abrupt and inappropriate job change, and a dramatic alteration of our personality style and approach to others (for example, an inability to modulate emotions). Extremes such as absenteeism or overinvolvement may not only cause personal problems but also represent poor coping strategies to those who see us as guides or mentors. As in the case of chronic stress, awareness of this potential problem is essential. Table 6 will help you detect signs of PTSD in yourself and others.

With this review of burnout, stress, and PTSD behind us, we now turn to what is entailed in a self-care protocol.

NOTES

1. Bode, R. (1993). *First you have to row a little boat.* New York: Warner.
2. Chekhov, A. Source unknown.
3. Sanders, L. (1986). *The Case of Lucy Bending.* New York: Berkley Books.
4. McLuhan, M. Source unknown.

5. Reinhold, B. B. (1997). *Toxic work: How to overcome stress, overload and burnout and revitalize your career.* New York: Plume.

6. Reinhold, B. B. (1997). *Toxic work: How to overcome stress, overload and burnout and revitalize your career.* New York: Plume.

7. Keller, P.A., & Ritt, L. (Eds.). (1984). *Innovations in clinical practice: A source book, Vol.* 3 (pp. 223). Sarasota, FL: Professional Resource Exchange.

8. Auden, W.H. (1976). "Introduction" to Dag Hammarskjold's *Markings*, NY: Knopf (p. ix).

9. Gill, J. (1980). Burnout: A growing threat in ministry. *Human Development, 1,* 24–25.

10. Kottler, J. (1989). *On being a therapist.* San Francisco: Jossey-Bass.

11. Foy, D., Drescher, K., Fits, A., & Kennedy, K. (2003). Post-traumatic stress disorder. In R. Wicks, R. Parsons, & D. Capps (Eds.), *Clinical handbook of pastoral counseling, Vol.* 3 (pp. 274–277). Mahwah, NJ: Paulist Press.

Personal Renewal: Creating and Tailoring Your Own Self-Care Protocol

Like many academics, I spent my young adult years postponing many of the small things that I knew would make me happy, including reading novels for pleasure, learning to cook, taking a photography class, and joining a gym. I would do all of these things when I had time—when I finished school, when I had a job, when I was awarded tenure, and so on. I was fortunate enough to realize that I would never have time unless I made the time. And then the rest of my life began.

Christopher Peterson,
A Primer in Positive Psychology

No one can say we haven't been told over and over again what we ought to do in order to build up our physical resilience. Exercise regularly. Eat the right foods. Take supplemental minerals and vitamins as necessary, especially folic acid, B12, and B6. Keep our weight within a healthy range. Have medical checkups annually. Get a good night's sleep. Don't smoke. Avoid drugs of abuse and use alcohol in moderation. Stretch. Get a massage now and then. Enjoy physical recreation such as hiking, swimming, tennis, and the like. Learn to relax. And if you are not already living by these guidelines, figure out why and do something.

Frederic Flach, *Resilience*

All of us seem to understand physical resilience, and what goes into maintaining it. But psychological resilience is still not well understood, and most of us don't realize how important it is to our well-being.

Care must be taken not to be so driven in our career or family life that everything else loses value and does not receive the attention it should. Although being a dedicated parent, sibling, child, friend, coworker, or citizen is a wonderful way to devote ourselves to the welfare of others, unless care is taken to ensure that the rest of our life is fulfilling and balanced, the way we live will become too narrow, limited, and eventually distorted. This can erode resilience and have a negative impact not only on ourselves, but eventually on our family and other interpersonal relationships as well.

In addition to workaholism and a narrowing of our horizons, in which outside interests, family, and even our own needs are neglected, there is the added problem of *denial*—a lack of clear awareness of the important issues or conflicts in one's life. Most people could probably deal with the dangers of stress and a poor quality of life if they were already aware of them. They would also take seriously the steps they must take to limit stress. Stress management includes some basic elements (see Table 7). So, it is worth taking a moment or two at this point to review them.

When we fail to take into consideration these basic elements of stress management—especially during those times when we are intensely involved with people and tasks at home and work—we may pay for this in terms of impaired psychological

Table 7   The Basics of Stress Management

Physical Health

1. *Sleep:* Without enough sleep, the quality of what you do will decrease; rising early requires going to bed at a reasonable hour.
2. *Food:* Eating three to five light meals, at a reasonable pace, and being mindful of the nutritional value of what you eat is one of the best ways to keep weight down and nourishment and energy up.
3. *Exercise:* Taking a fairly brisk walk each day is a good minimum exercise. Doing it on a consistent basis is better than some irregular or future extensive exercise plan which we fail at and feel guilty about.
4. *Leisure:* Relaxing with your feet up or being involved in activities that provide genuine enjoyment are not niceties of physical health. Rather, they are the undervalued but essential building blocks to good health. Leisure helps us "flow" with life's joys and problems in a more accepting philosophical way.
5. *Pacing:* Taking a little more time to get to a place makes the trip more relaxing; stopping every hour or hour and a half to get out of the car and stretch on long trips makes them a lot more enjoyable and helps increase stamina. Likewise, taking breaks when you feel the need increases your productivity. The important lesson here is to use any technique necessary to slow yourself down so you don't rush to the grave missing life's scenery along the way.

Psychological Stability

1. *Laughter:* If laughter is good medicine, then surely laughing at yourself is healing. We all tend to take ourselves too seriously. So, doing something about this can significantly reduce unnecessary stress and help improve your perspective on self and life.
2. *Values:* Know what is important and what isn't. By knowing what you believe to be really important, you can choose easily and well between alternatives.
3. *Control:* Be careful to discern between what you can control and what you can't. While worrying about something when it happens is natural, continuing to preoccupy yourself with it is not. When you

(continued)

Table 7 Continued

catch yourself worrying endlessly, tease yourself that you must be "the world's best worrier." Then plan what you can do about it, and let it go. If and when it comes up again; review the process until it lessens or stops. This technique may need a good deal of practice for it to "take root" in your attitude.

4. *Self-Appreciation:* Reflect on what gifts have been given you, recall them each day in detail—even making a list can be helpful—and be grateful for them by promising to nurture and share them in a generous way, without attachment to the outcome of your actions. At the same time, maintain awareness of your successes so you can appreciate your own good work. Remember not to focus too narrowly on the end result. We often fail to notice and value all the good we do along the way.

5. *Involvement . . . Not Over-Involvement:* Be active in what you feel is meaningful (the kind of things you would be pleased to reflect on at the very end of life—not necessarily those things that others might feel are impressive or important). Assertiveness on your part both to volunteer to be involved in what you believe is good and to say no to demands that aren't, is also an essential part of increasing your involvement in stimulating activities and curbing (wherever possible) ones that are personally draining.

6. *Support Group:* Have people in your life who care; contact them frequently by phone and in writing as well as in person. Ideally, among this group should include a variety of psychologically healthy friends who can challenge, support, encourage, teach, and make you laugh.

7. *Escape:* There are times when we should "run away" because facing things directly in all of our relationships all the time would be debilitating. To do this you can use novels, breaks during the day, movies, walks, hobbies (fishing, bicycle riding, etc.).

8. *Be Spontaneous:* A small creative action or change during the day or week can make life much more fun. This is a lot more practical than waiting for a yearly vacation.

9. *Be Careful of Negativity:* Often we hear negative comments like thunder and praise like a whisper. Use self-talk to catch your own negative tendencies (to see things in black-and-white terms, to exaggerate the negative, to let one negative event contaminate the whole day or week,

Table 7   Continued

or to discount other positive events). Then answer these thoughts with more accurate positive ones. For example, if you feel slightly depressed and check your thinking, you may see that because one thing went wrong today, you are saying to yourself that you are really a failure at what you do. By recognizing this exaggeration as nonsense, you can tell yourself more correctly that you made a mistake, not that you are a mistake! Following this, you can then recall successes you have had and bring to mind the faces of those who have been grateful for your presence in their lives. This will show you the face of love in the world and help break the back of any negative thinking that is influencing you at the time. Remember, negative thinking takes a good deal of energy. Stop it, and a great deal of energy will be freed up for growth and enjoyment.

10. *Check Your Individual Balance in the Areas of:*
    • Stimulation and quiet
    • Reflection and action
    • Work and leisure
    • Self-care and care of others
    • Self-improvement and patience
    • Future aspirations and present positive realities
    • Involvement and detachment

and physical health, not to mention the havoc it can wreak on those around us. Moreover, if we don't pay attention to our stress immediately, we eventually will. The problem with "eventually" is that, as with many psychophysical disorders in which psychological stress can produce physical changes over time, damage can occur so quietly over time that it can become irreversible (e.g. shingles after age 50). At that point, even when the stress is reduced in our lives and self-care is enriched, the physical harm already done can have chronic implications for the rest of our life.

Another reality that all of us must deal with in terms of ongoing stress is that the self is limited. It has only so much energy. If it is not renewed, then depletion will take place. Too often we don't avail ourselves of the type of activities that truly renew us. When this occurs we run a greater risk that we will unnecessarily lose perspective and burn out, which is not only sad for us but for the people in our lives who count on us.

TAKING RESPONSIBILITY FOR YOURSELF

Sometimes it takes a rude awakening for us to realize how far we have drifted from a balanced life. I can vouch for this personally and recall a conversation a number of years ago with a very close friend who was in his early forties and was dying of brain cancer. He was outrageous and we constantly teased one another. Even though he was dying, this did not stop.

He had been living in New York and I hadn't seen much of him in the years since I was the best man at his wedding. When he was hospitalized in Philadelphia to undergo experimental treatment, I visited him. When I came to visit he had already been there for almost two weeks, and when I inquired about his health he shared a summary of his condition, which included loss of short-term memory. So, I said to him: "You mean you can't remember what happened yesterday?" He said: "No."

Then I smiled and said: "So, you don't remember me coming in and sitting here with you each day for five hours for the
past two weeks?" He looked at me, hesitated for a second or
two, grinned widely, and said . . . well I can't share exactly what
he said . . . but we both had a good laugh over it.

One of the things he did surprise me with, though, was a
question that really helped me put my activities into perspective.
He asked: "What good things are you doing now?" As I started
to launch into an obsessive (naturally well-organized) list of my
recent academic and professional accomplishments, he inter-
rupted me by saying: "No, not that stuff. I mean what really
good things have you done? When have you gone fishing last?
Who is in your circle of friends, and what do you talk about
with them? What museums have you visited lately? What good
movies have you seen in the past month?" The "good things"
he was speaking about while dying were different from what
I thought about, in my arrogant good health. Unfortunately,
I have a lot of company in this regard.

Naturally, what makes up a self-care protocol or personal
renewal program varies from person to person. It also differs
according to the person's stage of life. As psychologist Ellen
Baker notes:

There are many different ways to practice self-care. No one
model exists in terms of definition, meaning, significance, or
application. Differences between individuals relate to personal history, gender, and personality, and within-individual

differences relate to developmental stage, or changing needs. Such differences influence the substance and process of self-care. For one person at a particular stage of life, self-care might involve maintaining a very active schedule and hiring a housekeeper. For another person, or for the same person at a different stage, self-care might involve considerable amounts of quiet, uncommitted personal time and tending one's own home.[1]

Since such a list needs to be tailored, it is helpful to have a large pool of possibilities from which to choose. Use the list below to spur your thinking around what could comprise a self-care protocol in your own case. Recognize that spending time on self-care is part of the self-respect needed to experience a richer quality of life.

ELEMENTS OF A SELF-CARE PROTOCOL OR PERSONAL RENEWAL PROGRAM

There are basic elements of a self-care protocol or renewal program that most of us need in order to replenish ourselves and reinforce our resilience on an ongoing basis. It really doesn't require too much to take a step back from our work or family routine to become refreshed in order to regain perspective. Some of the basic elements might include:

- Quiet walks by yourself
- Time and space for meditation

- Spiritual and recreational reading—including the diaries and biographies of others whom you admire
- Some light exercise
- Opportunities to laugh offered by movies, cheerful friends, a regular card game
- A hobby such as gardening or knitting
- Phone calls to family and friends who inspire and tease you
- Involvement in projects that renew you
- Listening to music you enjoy

Other simple aspects of self-care that help to broaden our renewal program might include:

- Visiting a park or hiking
- Having family or friends over for dinner or evening coffee
- Going to a mega-bookstore to have coffee and a scone, and taking time to peruse the magazines
- Shopping for little things that would be fun to have but don't cost a lot
- Taking a bath rather than a quick shower
- Daydreaming
- Forming a "dining club" in which you go out once a month for lunch with a friend or sibling
- E-mailing friends
- Listening to a book on tape
- Reading poetry out loud
- Staying in bed later than usual on a day off
- Having a leisurely discussion with your spouse over morning coffee in bed

- Watching an old movie
- Making love
- Buying and reading a magazine you have never read before
- Planting a small garden with bright cheery flowers
- Telephoning someone you haven't spoken to in ages
- Buying and playing a new CD of a singer or musician you enjoy
- Taking a short walk (without using a Walkman) before and after work or during lunchtime
- Going to a diner or small restaurant and having a cup of tea and a piece of pie
- Going on a weekend retreat at a local spirituality center or hotel that has extensive grounds so you can take time out to walk, reflect, eat when you want, read as long as you'd like, or just renew yourself
- Arranging to spend a couple of days by yourself in your own home without family or friends present just to lounge around and be alone without a schedule or the needs and agendas of others
- Journaling each day as a way of unwinding

You'll notice that these are all very simple things. The important point is to recognize the serious need to intentionally and spontaneously make room for these elements in our schedule so they represent a constant, significant portion of the time we have available each day/week/month/year. In their book *Self-Nurture* (primarily written for women but filled with good suggestions for anyone concerned about their own welfare),

Alice Domar and Henry Dreher refer to the space we have available as a "time pie." They suggest that once we prepare our list of self-care activities, we then see how much time we actually allot for what we say we are interested in doing for ourselves. They write:

> Now compare your list . . . with your time pie. How much time is indicated on the pie for any of the activities listed? Of course, there may be pastimes on your list that you wouldn't do that frequently, like going to a comedy club. But others, like daydreaming or reading, might ideally be part of a typical day. Do these activities show up on our time pie? Many women who follow this exercise discover that there is *no* time on their pie for any of the . . . items. Others count the time spent on purely joyful activity in minutes rather than hours. This can be a shocking revelation, one that motivates some women to radically transform the way they spend their time.[2]

QUESTIONS TO PONDER IN DEVELOPING YOUR SELF-CARE PROTOCOL/PERSONAL RENEWAL PROGRAM

Time is a very precious commodity for most of us. How we allot it, what takes precedence, and with whom we spend it, all say a great deal about us and the way we live our lives. In the words of the Dalai Lama in his book *The Path to Tranquility*, "It is very wrong for people to feel deeply sad when they lose some money, yet when they waste the precious moments of their lives they do not have the slightest feeling of repentance."[3] Yet "waste" for some people sometimes means the wrong thing. The feeling may be that if I take out time for myself, this leisure period is not really "time well spent." Instead, it is seen as being almost wrong, given all the demands we have. With this philosophy, at the very least, leisure time must be earned by conducting a stretch of long hours of service without any rejuvenating break. To counter this dysfunctional philosophy, we must explore the options available to us for developing a self-care protocol inventory, while at the same time recognizing it is not a nicety of life but a necessary source of constant renewal.

Once we have developed and reflected upon such a list of self-care elements, how it is then used is also crucial. At this point, the challenging question that presents itself is: *How do we formulate a self-care protocol that we are likely to use beneficially and regularly rather than in spurts?* And so, to ensure that an ongoing systematic program is in place, first we must direct a number of questions to ourselves. This is to avoid the dangers of, on the one hand, being unrealistic in developing a protocol and, on the other, of not being creative and expansive enough. Such questions can also help set the stage for Designing a Personal

Self-Care Protocol (as outlined in Table 8 at the end of the chapter). Included among these preliminary questions are:

- When someone says, "self-care," what image comes to mind? What are the positive and negative aspects of this image? In terms of importance and how realistic it is to develop your own self-care protocol, where do you stand?
- In terms of self-care, what is unique in your case given your field of employment or family situation?
- How do you balance your time alone to renew your energy, reflect on your life, and clear your thinking with the time you spend with those who challenge, support, and make you laugh?
- Self-care and self-knowledge go hand in hand. What types of activities (structured reflection at the end of a day, informal debriefing of oneself during the drive home, journaling, mentoring, therapy, spiritual guidance, reading, etc.) are you involved in which will help you develop a systematic and ongoing analysis of how you are progressing in life?
- What types of exercise (walking, working out, swimming, etc.) do you enjoy and feel would be realistic for you to be involved in on a regular basis?
- Who in your circle of friends provides you with encouragement, challenge, perspective, laughter, and inspiration? How do you ensure that you have ongoing contact with him or her?

- The balance between work and leisure, professional time and personal time, varies from person to person. What is the ideal balance for you? What steps have you taken to ensure that this balance is kept?
- Self-care involves not getting pulled into the dramatic emotions, fears, and anger that may pervade our home and work settings. What are the self-care elements that support a healthy sense of detachment?
- Being too conservative or procrastinating at one end of the spectrum versus acting rashly or impulsively at the other end, are extremes that can be dangerous. How do you maintain a sense of balance that prevents behavior at either extreme?
- How do you prepare for change since it is such a natural and constant part of everyone's life?
- What is the best way you can find balance between stimulation and time spent in silence and solitude? Avoid constant stimulation as well as isolation and preoccupation with self.
- How do you process "unfinished business" (failures, duplicity in one's relationships, past negative events, hurts, fears, lost relationships, and so on) in your life so that you have enough energy to deal with the challenges and appreciate the joys in front of you?
- What do you number among the stable forces in your life that are anchors for your own sense of well-being and self-care?

- In what way do you ensure that your goals are challenging and high, but not unrealistic and deflating?
- What self-care steps do you have to take because of your gender or race that others of a different race or gender don't have to take?
- How has your past experience set habits in motion that make self-care a challenge in some ways?
- What self-care steps are more important at this stage of your life than they were at earlier life stages?
- What emotional and physical "red flags" are you aware of which indicate that you must take certain self-care steps so as not to burn out, violate boundaries, "medicate" yourself in unhealthy ways (with alcohol, for example), withdraw when you shouldn't, verbally attack family or colleagues, or drown yourself in work?
- What do you *already* do in terms of self-care? In each of the following areas, what have you found to be most beneficial with regard to physical health, interactions with a circle of friends, professionally, financially, psychologically, and spiritually?
- What is *the next step* you need to take in developing your self-care protocol? How do you plan to bring this about?
- Are your holidays and vacations appropriately spaced and sufficient for your needs? What is the most renewing way for you to spend this time?
- Are you also conscious of the need for "mini-holidays" involving a brief tea or coffee break, a short walk, playing

with the children in the evening, or visiting one's friends or parents? Practicing a putt in your office or living room, shopping, or casting with a fly rod in a neighborhood field?

Reflecting on these questions periodically, and responding honestly to all of them, can improve personal resilience and self-knowledge in ways that aid in preventing burnout. They also can increase sensitivity to how we live our life in a way that enables us to both flourish personally and become more faithful and passionate professionally. Once again, the way we move through the day depends a great deal on our personality style. *Burnout is not necessarily from the amount of work, but how we perceive it and interact with people as we pursue our work.* Some people complain that they are so busy that they don't have time to breathe. Others with the same intense schedule reflect on how happy they are that they are involved in so many challenging projects.

Some of us love exercise and thrive on it. Others are more sedentary. All of us though, want to be physically healthy. Not everyone likes outdoor activities and vacations packed with touring new sights and experiencing adventures. Some would prefer the backyard, a leisurely walk, an artist's easel, a good book, or a familiar restaurant. But all of us need time away at different points.

The differences among us are many. That is why each self-care protocol or personal renewal program, if it is to be both realistic and effective, is unique in its composition.

The important point to note is that we must have a self-care protocol in place that we can employ as a daily guide, while being alert to rationalizations and excuses for not doing it. Not to have such a personal renewal program may court disaster for both our personal and professional lives. It is also, at its core, an act of profound disrespect for the gift of life we have been given.

When we have true self-respect that is evidenced by a sound self-care protocol, it can also be transformative for us. It is important to keep in mind that its benefits are not just for us. One of the greatest gifts we can share with those who are close to us is a sense of our own peace and resilience. But we can't share what we don't have. It is as simple as that.

Also, we need to recognize that when we speak about self-care and self-nurturing, we are not referring here to another intense program that just adds more stress to life in the name of reducing it. Once again, I quote Domar and Dreher:

> True body-nurture absolutely includes physical activity and sound nutrition, but not compulsive exercise and onerous dietary restriction. True body-nurture is also much more than exercise and nutrition. It includes the following actions and ideas:
> - Deep diaphragmatic breathing
> - A regular practice of relaxation
> - Cognitive restructuring of body-punishing thoughts into thoughts of compassion and forgiveness

- Delight in the sensual and sexual pleasures of the body
- A sane, balanced, non-shame-based relationship with food
- Health-promoting behaviors, such as stopping smoking, alcohol in moderation, and regular visits to the doctor for preventive care
- A profound regard for the sacredness of the body, including all its functions, imperfections, idiosyncrasies, and wonders[4]

Such an overall approach to physical health along with the other approaches mentioned thus far will clearly benefit us. They will also help us develop attitudes and behaviors that will improve psychological health as well as increase personal and professional well-being.

Before closing this brief treatment of the topic of self-care, a basic broad-based questionnaire designed to aid in the development of our own self-care protocol (Table 8) is now provided. It will serve as a summary of the contents of this chapter and when filled out is designed to provide a succinct list of items we feel should be part of a self-care protocol. In addition, completing and reflecting upon it alone, with a mentor, or in a group of colleagues, can be revealing and instructive as to what areas might need more or less emphasis in the future. This allows us then to create and design a renewal program that particularly suits us. This personalizing of the protocol, in itself, will help to uncover and overcome the resistance that normally accompanies general one-size-fits-all self-care programs created by others. *Bon chance!*

Table 8   Designing a Personal Self-Care Protocol

This material is for your own use. There is a tendency on some people's part to be quick, terse, or global in their responses. Such approaches, while natural, limit the helpfulness of completing this questionnaire to gain as full an awareness as possible of your current profile and the personal goals you plan to develop for a realistic, rich, and balanced self-care program. Consequently, in preparing this personally-designed protocol, the more clear, specific, complete, imaginative, and realistic your responses are to the questions provided, the more practical and beneficial the material will be.

1. List healthy *nutritional practices* that you currently have in place.

2. What are specific realistic ways to improve your habit/style of eating and drinking (of alcoholic beverages)?

3. What *physical exercise* do you presently get and when is it scheduled during the week?

4. What changes in your schedule in terms of time, frequency, and variety with respect to exercise do you wish to make?

5. Where are the periods for reflection, quiet time, meditation, mini-breaks alone, opportunities to center yourself, and personal debriefing times now in your schedule?

6. Given your personality style, family life, and work situation, what changes would you like to make in your schedule to make it more intentional and balanced with respect to processing what comes to the fore in your time spent alone or in silence?

7. How much, what type, and how deeply and broadly do you read at this point?

8. What would you like to do to increase variety or depth in your reading, research, and continuing-education pursuits?

(continued)

Table 8   Continued

9. Below list activities present in your nonworking schedule not previously noted above. Alongside of the frequency/time, list changes to this schedule that you feel would further enrich you personally and professionally as well as have a positive impact, in turn, on your family, colleagues, and overall social network.

Activities	Frequency/ Time Now Allotted	Planned Change/ Improvement
Leisure time with:		
Spouse/ Significant Other Children Parents Family Members Friends		
Going to Movies		
Watching TV		
Visiting Museums		
Sports		
Attending Concerts/ Plays		
Listening to Music		
Hiking, Biking, Walking, or Swimming		

Table 8 Continued

Activities	Frequency/ Time Now Allotted	Planned Change/ Improvement
Phone Calls to Family and Friends		
Hobbies (Gardening, coin collecting, etc.)		
Dining Out		
Shopping		
Visiting Libraries, Bookstores, Coffee Shops		
E-mailing Friends		
Making Love		
Journaling		
Continuing Education		
Vacations		
Long Weekends Away		
Meditation/ Reflection/ Sitting Zazen		
Religious Rituals		

(continued)

Table 8 Continued

Activities	Frequency/ Time Now Allotted	Planned Change/ Improvement
Leisurely Baths		
Message		
Other Activities Not Listed Above:		

_____

_____

_____

_____

10 What are the ways you process strong emotions (anger, anxiety, deep sadness, confusion, fear, emotional "highs," or the desire to violate boundaries for reasons of personal/sexual/financial/power gratifications)?

11 Where in your schedule do you regularly undertake such emotional processing/unpacking?

12 What would you like to do to change the extent and approaches you are now using for self-analysis/debriefing of self?

13 Who comprises the interpersonal anchors in your life?

14 What do you feel is lacking in your network of friends?

15 What are some reasonable initiatives you wish to undertake to have a richer network?

Table 8 Continued

16 What are your sleep/rest habits now?

17 If you are not getting enough sleep/rest, what are some realistic ways to ensure you get more?

Note: This is just a partial questionnaire. Please feel free to include, analyze, and develop a plan for improvement and integration of other aspects of self-care. Also, review your answers at different points to see what resistances to change come up, and how you can face them in new creative ways by yourself or with the help of a friend, colleague, mentor, or professional counselor or therapist.

NOTES

1. Baker, E. (2003). *Caring for ourselves: A therapist's guide to personal and professional well-being.* Washington, DC: American Psychological Association.

2. Domar, A., & Dreher, H. (2000). *Self-nurture: Learning to care for yourself as effectively as you care for everyone else.* New York: Penguin.

3. Dalai Lama. (2000). *The path to tranquility.* New York: Penguin.

4. Domar, A., & Dreher, H. (2000). *Self-nurture: Learning to care for yourself as effectively as you care for everyone else.* New York: Penguin.

A POWERFUL HEALING
COMBINATION: FRIENDSHIP,
RESILIENCE, AND COMPASSION

It is in the shelter of each other that the people live.

PEIG SAYERS

*The more self-absorbed we are, the less there is to find
absorbing. To have no real involvement with others, no
identification with them, no interest—in other words, to lack
compassion—is to shrink one's world down to the cramped
precincts within one's own skill. And there is not enough there
for one long solo trip in a car without a tape deck, let alone
for a lifetime.*

CORNELIUS "NEAL" PLANTINGA, JR.

*Regardless of our age and how secure and confident we feel, if we
are to strengthen and maintain our optimism and resilience it is
essential that we interact with people who accept us and from
whom we gather strength . . . we all thrive on its presence.*

JULIUS SEGAL

One of the key aspects of self-care that is worth special
emphasis when we are focusing on remaining resilient
is to have a well-rounded circle of friends. Anthropologist
Margaret Meade once noted that "One of the oldest human

needs is having someone to wonder where you are when you don't come home at night." Psychology has long emphasized the need for an excellent interpersonal network as a major element of health and happiness. As Ellen Baker notes in her book on self-care for psychologists:

> To care for our self in relationship with others, we must actively nurture our relationships with our significant other, children, family of origin, friends, and colleagues. Connecting with others beyond our immediate circle of relationships can be equally important; participation in community organizations can help us feel connected to a larger whole . . . The quality of our relationships, more than the quantity, is key. In both our personal and professional lives our best relationships are those in which we can be as close to our true self as possible.[1]

For all major spiritual traditions, "community" is also an essential element. Yet, as Baker has just noted, *who* is in that community is just as significant as the recognition that we should be part of one. As psychologist and spiritual writer Henri Nouwen recognizes:

> We can take a lot of physical and even mental pain when we know that it truly makes us a part of the life we live together in the world. But when we feel cut off from the human family, we quickly lose heart.[2]

An absence of at least one significant friend may even have serious health consequences:

Redford Williams, M.D., of Duke University, tracked almost 1,400 men and women who underwent coronary angiograms and were found to have at least one severely blocked coronary artery. After five years, those who were unmarried and who did not have at least one close confidante were over three times more likely to have died than people who were married, had one or more confidantes, or both.[3]

In my own work, both personal and professional, I have found that for the circle to be rich we need, at the very least, four "types" or "voices" present (since one friend may play more than one beneficial role at different points in our lives). These four types of friends are the *prophet*, the *cheerleader*, the *harasser*, and the *guide*. By having these "voices" in our lives, we increase our chances of maintaining a sense of perspective, openness, and balance.

THE PROPHET

The first of these voices which helps us maintain balance and have a sense of openness is the one I refer to as the prophet. Contrary to what one might imagine, prophetic friends need not look or behave any differently than other types of persons who are close to us. The true prophet's voice is often quiet and fleeting, but nonetheless strong. She or he is living an honest and courageous life guided by truth and compassion. Such persons are trying to live out the truth, and whether knowingly or not, they follow the advice of Gandhi: "Let our first act every morning be this resolve: I shall not fear anyone on earth . . . I shall not bear ill-will toward anyone. I shall conquer untruth by truth and in resisting untruth, I shall put up with all suffering."

The message of prophets often involves discomfort or pain, not masochistic pain but real pain. Often they do not directly produce conflict. Instead, like leaders in the nonviolent movement, they "merely" set the stage for it, as is pointed out in the following words of Martin Luther King, Jr.:

> We who engage in nonviolent, direct action are not the creators of tension. We merely bring to the surface the hidden tension that is already alive. We bring it out in the open, where it can be seen and dealt with. Like a boil that can never be cured so long as it is covered up but must be opened with all its ugliness to the natural medicines of air and light, injustice must be exposed, with all the tension its exposure creates, to the light of human conscience and the air of national opinion before it can be cured.[4]

Having someone prophetic in our lives is never easy. No matter how positive we may believe the ultimate consequences will be for us, many of us still shy away from prophetic messages and would readily agree with Henry David Thoreau: "If you see someone coming to do you a good deed, run for your life!" However, to seek comfort in lieu of the truth may mean that in an effort to avoid pain, we will also avoid responding to opportunities of real value, real life. We will merely exist and eventually die without having ever really lived. Prophets point! They point to the fact that it doesn't matter whether pleasure or pain is involved, the only thing that matters is that we seek to see and live "the truth" because only it will set us free.

In doing this, prophets challenge us to look at how we are living our lives, to ask ourselves: "To what voices am I listening when I form my attitudes and take my actions each day?"

THE CHEERLEADER

Ironically, one of the most controversial suggestions I might make with respect to friendship is to suggest we all need "cheerleaders." Some might say that to encourage this type of friend is to run the risk of narcissism and denial. However, to balance the prophetic voices we also need unabashed, enthusiastic, unconditional acceptance by certain people in our lives. Prophecy can and should instill appropriate guilt to break through the crusts of our denial. But guilt cannot sustain us for long. While guilt will push us to do good things because they are right, love encourages us to do the right thing because it is natural.

We can't go it alone. We need a balance of support. We need encouragement and acceptance as much as we need the criticism and feedback that are difficult to hear. Burnout is always around the corner when we don't have people who are ready to encourage us, see our gifts clearly, and be there for us when our involvement with people, their sometimes unrealistic demands, and our own crazy expectations for ourselves threaten to pull us down. So, while having buoyantly supportive friends may seem like a luxury, make no mistake about it—it is a necessity that is not to be taken lightly. The "interpersonal roads" over time are strewn with well-meaning helpers who tried to survive without such support. Encouragement is a gift that should be treasured in today's stressful, anxious, complex world because the seeds of involvement and the seeds of burnout are the same. To be involved is to risk. And to risk without the presence of solidly supportive friends is foolhardy and dangerous.

THE HARASSER

When singer-activist Joan Baez was asked her opinion about the contemplative monk and writer Thomas Merton, one of the things she said was that he was different from many of the phony gurus she had encountered in her travels. She said that although Merton took important things seriously in his life, he didn't take himself too seriously. She indicated that he knew how to laugh at situations and particularly at himself. "Harassers" help us to laugh at ourselves and to avoid the emotional burnout that results from having the unrealistic expectation that people will always follow our guidance or appreciate what we do for them. This type of friend helps us regain and maintain perspective (so we don't unnecessarily waste valuable energy). They often do this by gentle teasing. This is truly a gift for which we can be thankful.

GUIDES

The three types of friends we've looked at thus far are each part of a necessary community. The prophet enhances our sense of single-mindedness. The cheerleader generously showers us with the support we feel we need. The harasser encourages us to maintain a sense of proper perspective. Complementing these three is a cluster that, for lack of a better name, shall be referred to as "guides." Such persons listen to us carefully and don't accept the "manifest content" (what we say and do) as being equal to the "total content" (our actual intentions plus our statements and actions). Instead, they search and look for nuances in what we share with them to help us to uncover some of the "voices" that are unconsciously guiding our lives, especially the ones that make us hesitant, anxious, fearful, and willful.

To determine whether or how these voices are present in our lives, several questions seeking further information about the composition of our circle of friends might be helpful:

- Do I have friends with whom I can simply be myself?
- What type of friends do I value most? Why?
- What do I feel are the main qualities of friendship?
- List and briefly describe the friends who are now in my life.
- Describe ones who are no longer alive or present to me now but who have made an impact on my life. Why do I think they made such a difference in my life?
- Among my circle of friends, who are my personal heroes or role models?
- Who are the prophets in my life? In other words, who confronts me with the question: To what voices am I responding in life?
- Who help me to see my relationships, mission in life, and self-image more clearly? How do they accomplish this?
- Who encourage me in a genuine way through praise and a nurturing spirit?
- Who tease me into gaining a new perspective when I am too preoccupied or tied up in myself?
- When and with whom do I play different (prophetic, supportive, etc.) roles as a friend? How do people receive such interactions?

Having a healthy and balanced circle of friends can help ward off stress and benefit our personal and professional growth. This is an obvious reality. The important point here is that with some attention to this area, we can immeasurably improve the role that encouraging, challenging, and guiding friendships can have in our lives. In turn, it can also provide an impetus to fill similar roles for others, which can also be a deeply rewarding experience for us.

BECOMING A RESILIENT AND COMPASSIONATE FRIEND TO OTHERS

A life that is filled with many requests from family, friends, and coworkers can at times be overwhelming. We often focus too much attention on the challenges involved while neglecting to recognize the rewarding and renewing aspects of living compassionately. As Vietnamese Zen Roshi Thich Nhat Hanh recognized when reflecting upon his helping role during a very dark time in his own country and life:

> During the war, we were so busy helping the wounded that we sometimes forgot to smell the flowers. Night has a very pleasant smell [here], especially in the country. But we would forget to pay attention to the smell of mint, coriander, thyme, and sage.[5]

But as psychologist Mihály Csikszentmihalyi points out, there is something uniquely human about gaining sustenance or happiness by being part of activities or causes that go beyond our own:

> . . . human beings are not just self-serving entities, but are rewarded also by a holistic principle of motivation. In other words, our well-being is enhanced when we devote energy to goals that go beyond the momentary and the selfish. We feel happier pursuing short-term goals than no goals at all; when pursing long-term goals rather than short-term ones; when working to better ourselves rather than just having pleasure; and we feel happier when working for the well-being of another person, group, or larger entity as opposed to just investing effort in self-focused goals. These relationships seem to hold both at the momentary level of experience, and also developmentally, over the life-span—so that persons who devote more time to hierarchically more complex goals are also, on the whole, happier.[6]

THE GIFT OF PRESENCE . . .
AND ITS DANGERS

Simple presence has a powerful healing value that children seem more aware of than many adults. The following story poignantly illustrates this:

> One day a woman's little girl arrived home late after school. The mother was so angry that she started to yell at her.

However, after about five minutes, she suddenly stopped and asked: "Why were you late anyway?"

The daughter replied: "Because I had to help another girl who was in trouble."

"Well, what did you do to help her?"

The daughter replied: "Oh, I sat down next to her and helped her cry."

A listening presence is quite simple, powerful, and healing. True listening in and of itself tells the person that I:

- Want to take the effort to know you and your situation better
- Am attending carefully so that I can provide feedback
- Will ask questions if I don't fully understand
- Am interested in helping open up new alternatives
- Will spend the time, energy, and effort to be creative so we can seek new perspectives and approaches by problem-solving together

A person who truly listens stands out because so few people take the time and have the openness to do so. I began thinking about this fact when I read the following tribute to Sir Laurence Olivier by Anthony Hopkins that appeared in the *New York Times* a number of years ago:

He came forward to shake my hand and I gave him my name. He gave me his full attention. This was an ability of his, to give his full, undivided attention to the moment, as if there were no past or future. Even in his "ordinariness" there was that one peculiar quality of concentration. This is what set him apart as an extraordinary human being: he never dismissed anything, he never disregarded anything. Everything held his attention.[7]

When we let people express their feelings without reacting with anxiety, just that act can be a balm for the soul. As beautiful and necessary as compassion is to experiencing a full life and helping others to raise the quality of their lives, there are dangers involved for those who reach out. In an article on satisfaction among doctors, researchers found that "higher perceived stress [was] associated with lower satisfaction levels [and were] related to greater intentions [by the physician] to quit, decrease work hours, change specialty, or leave direct patient care. One can see here the powerful effect of the combination of job stress and dissatisfaction. So powerful, in fact, that some of these highly trained, committed professionals may leave their practice situations while others cope by decreasing work hours, changing practice emphasis or leaving direct patient care."[8] This "giving up the good fight" can obviously be the case for us as well if we are not careful. And so, a balanced relationship between a steady commitment to being compassionate and a firm commitment to personal resilience should be our goal.

President John F. Kennedy used to tell the following story about one of his favorite authors:

> Frank O'Connor, the Irish author, tells in one of his books how as a boy, he and his friends would make their way across the countryside and when they came to an orchard wall that

seemed too high and too doubtful to try, and too difficult to permit their voyage to continue, they would take off their hats and toss them over the wall—and then they had no choice but to follow them![9]

To make it over "the high walls" in life, we not only need a sound circle of friends, but must be willing to offer compassion and ourselves to others as well. Once again, this is not simply because it would be beneficial to them but also because our ultimate joy is tied to such acts of compassion. As humanitarian Albert Schweitzer once said, "I don't know what your destiny will be, but one thing I do know, the only ones among you who will be really happy are those who have sought and found how to serve."[10] And we can only serve others and society well if we can cultivate the resilient life.

SIGNATURE STRENGTHS, HAPPINESS, AND THE RESILIENT SELF

I believe that the highest success in living and the deepest emotional satisfaction comes from building and using your signature strengths.
MARTIN SELIGMAN,
Authentic Happiness

For most of their history, mental health professionals have focused on ameliorating suffering by primarily being concerned with the *negative* side of personality and distress. Therapies concentrated on disorders, not on deepening the good aspects of a person's life. But that focus is now shifting, and a number of researchers are beginning to expand into areas that look at how people cope well in today's stressful world. In turn, this has brought increased awareness of the value of *resilience*. By drawing attention to people's gifts, talents, and virtues—all of which are essential for inner strength and a good quality of life—people can then build upon what is good and not merely focus all energies on correcting what is problematic.

According to Martin Seligman, who initiated the contemporary positive psychology movement:

The field of positive psychology at the subjective level is about positive subjective experience: well-being and satisfaction (past); flow, joy, the sensual pleasures, and happiness (present); and constructive cognitions about the future— optimism, hope, and faith. At the individual level it is about positive personal traits—the capacity for love and vocation, courage, interpersonal skill, aesthetic sensibility, perseverance, forgiveness, originality, future-mindedness, high talent, and wisdom . . . Psychology is not just the study of disease, weakness, and damage; it also is the study of strength and virtue. Treatment is not just fixing what is wrong; it also is building what is right . . . the major strides in prevention have largely come from a perspective focused on systematically building competency, not correcting weakness . . . This, then, is the general stance of positive psychology toward prevention. It claims that there is a set of buffers against psychopathology: the positive human traits.[11]

But Seligman is also concerned about the tendency to interpret behaviors, even the positive actions people take, as being the result of compensations or defenses rather than to see them in a positive light. He refers to this as the "rotten-to-the-core doctrine" and provides a wonderful illustration of this in his popular and helpful book *Authentic Happiness*:

> The rotten-to-the-core doctrine also pervades the understanding of human nature in the arts and social sciences. Just one example of thousands is *No Ordinary Time*, a gripping history of Franklin and Eleanor Roosevelt written by Doris Kearns Goodwin, one of the great living political scientists. Musing on the question of why Eleanor dedicated so much of her life to helping people who were black, poor, or disabled, Goodwin decides that it was "to compensate for her mother's narcissism and her father's alcoholism." Nowhere does Goodwin consider the possibility that deep down, Eleanor Roosevelt was pursuing virtue. Motivations like exercising fairness or pursuing duty are ruled out as fundamental: there *must* be some covert, negative motivation that underpins goodness if the analysis is to be academically respectable.
>
> I cannot say this too strongly . . . *there is not a shred of evidence that strength and virtue are derived from negative motivation.*[12]

Seligman's findings and that of other researchers in the positive psychology area are important in terms of how people view themselves professionally and personally. Their insights allow us to question ourselves in a completely new way, to view our strengths and virtues rather than our faults. At the end of this chapter I provide a questionnaire for self-reflection on personal strengths and virtues (see Table 10). The goal in reviewing these questions is to balance the tendency to look *solely* at our shortcomings and mistakes with an opportunity to appreciate our talents and gifts as well. Such an undertaking balances and enhances interpretations of past and present motivations and actions and instills one with a greater sense of optimism and hope. The rationale is that this more balanced attitude toward debriefing has the potential to be the most significant part of the reflective process we undertake during the day, week, month, year, and periodic life-span changes that we move through. Moreover, as we will see in the following pages, positive emotions can expand the repertoire of our approach to life.

INTRODUCING POSITIVE PSYCHOLOGY

Several points made by psychologist Christopher Peterson—in what I have found to be one of the most engaging, succinct, yet complete introductions to the area (*A Primer in Positive Psychology*)—set the stage for considering the scope and relevance for us of positive psychology. According to Peterson:

> **Positive psychology** is the scientific study of what goes right in life . . . It is a newly christened approach within psychology that takes seriously as a subject matter those things that make life worth living. . . positive psychology does not deny the valleys. Its signature premise is more nuanced but nonetheless important: What is good about life is as genuine as what is bad and therefore deserves equal attention from psychologists.[13]

Positive psychology then is not a psychological cosmetic that covers up the real blemishes of life. Nor is it an emotional cortisone that temporarily eliminates unpleasant life experiences that all of us must face. Instead, it is a more dynamic way of viewing ourselves that broadens our horizons rather than merely focusing our outlook on the negative, on only things that need fixing.

To begin looking at our strengths, we need a framework for examining the "good life." Once again, to use Peterson's words: "We can parse the field into three related topics: (a) positive subjective experiences (happiness, pleasure, gratification, fulfillment), (b) positive individual traits (strengths of character, talents, interests, values), and (c) positive institutions (families, schools, businesses, communities, societies)."[14]

THE LINK BETWEEN HAPPINESS
AND RESILIENCE

As Carr notes in his fine work *Positive Psychology: The Science of Happiness and Human Strengths,* "Evidence from developmental and laboratory studies shows that positive mood states help people build enduring personal resources. Developmental studies of securely and insecurely attached children show that the former exhibit greater persistence, flexibility and resourcefulness in solving problems than the latter. They also show greater exploratory behavior in novel situations and develop superior cognitive maps. Adults with secure attachment styles are more curious and open to new information than those with insecure attachment styles. Educational studies of children show that children in positive mood states learn faster . . . In view of [the] evidence which shows that positive emotions can [also] facilitate creativity and problem solving, it is not surprising that happiness also increases work productivity."[15]

These findings are crucial in pointing to the link between using our strengths at work or with our hobbies and that which makes us happy. It's not surprising that we are most happy, and most productive, when we are using our signature strengths. Accordingly, it is important to become more aware of what activities lead to happiness for us and to ask ourselves questions such as:

• With what type of situations do I get so wonderfully immersed in that I seem to lose track of time?

- What kinds of challenges would I want more of in my job or personal life?
- What are some of the skills that would help me feel less under stress in my interactions with others at work and home?
- When do I worry the most about what coworkers and family will think about me? What can I do to lessen this?
- What experiences do I enjoy the most, occupationally and personally? Why is this the case, and what can I do to expand the possibility of them happening?
- What type of challenges are:

  Below my skill level?

  Even with my skill level?

  Above my skill level?

The interesting finding is that happiness makes us more resilient. The benefits of happiness extend beyond just the enjoyment of good feelings. In fact, research indicates that joy pays major physical and psychological dividends.

Compared to their dour counterparts, happy people:

- Are healthier and live longer
- Are more productive at work and have higher incomes
- Are more tolerant and creative, and make decisions more easily
- Select more challenging goals, persist longer, and perform better in a variety of laboratory tasks
- Demonstrate greater empathy, have close friends, and enjoy better marriages[16]

Psychologist Barbara Frederickson has also found a relationship between positive emotions and joy and how this enables individuals to build a variety of personal resources, including physical (skills, health, longevity), social (friendships, social support networks), intellectual (expert knowledge, intellectual complexity), and psychological (resilience, optimism, creativity) resources. Her theory emphasizes that positive emotions strengthen resources that are drawn on throughout life to improve coping and improve our odds of survival.

Perhaps, then, Robert Louis Stevenson was right when he said, "There is no duty we so underrate as the duty to be happy. By being happy we sow anonymous benefits upon the world."

TAKING THE TIME TO LEARN OUR SIGNATURE STRENGTHS

Table 9 provides some guidance on how to begin thinking about your own signature strengths as well as making time for activities that build resilience. As you read each point, reflect on whether or how it is in sync with your own philosophy of life and current approach to leisure activities.

The primary goal then of studying positive psychology is to provide a reflective grid that focuses us on *those positive experiences, events, behaviors, cognitions, gifts, talents, and conditions to be recalled,*

Table 9   Enhancing Happiness and Optimism, and in Turn, Resilience

The following simple suggestions are made in accordance with positive psychology research. By taking or reinforcing the following actions, you can strengthen your own sense of well-being, quality of life, and happiness in an array of ways which in turn will enhance resilience.

- Provide as much time to take stock of your gifts and talents as you do of your own shortcomings. Such an exercise can lead to healthy optimism as well as a clearer awareness of the strengths you have that you can bring to bear in a myriad of personal and occupational situations.

- Become involved in leisure activities that require interactions with others rather than simply being on your own. This will meet not only natural needs for community and service, but offer stimulation and all-consuming activities that can use our personal talents. When music and altruism are also present, these leisure experiences may be even more powerful since they provide aesthetic moments and a reinforcement of your value system which can positively affect your level of happiness.

- Although shopping can be fun and earning a good salary is rewarding, placing greater emphasis on the free gifts of life that are always before us can also immeasurably improve our quality of life and enable us to be a resilient and helpful presence to others. By enjoying the natural gifts that life offers us, we learn that being countercultural has great advantages. For instance, we begin to see that if we want more (material goods, fame, etc.), when we get it, we then look to getting even more. If we seek something different, after we experience it for a while, it becomes more of the same. Likewise, when we seek the so-called "perfect" in life that will supposedly make us secure and happy, we realize that we miss what we have already been granted by life. Research shows that after we earn a salary which meets our basic needs, additional money does little (if anything!) to improve our quality of life and our happiness. Remembering this simple proven fact can immeasurably reduce stress, increase happiness, and prevent inner resilience from being eroded by a future "purchase" of joy that always seems just beyond reach.

(continued)

Table 9   Continued

- Cultivate a sense of gratitude by remembering to compare your life with those who have less than you have, instead of focusing only on those who seem to have more than you do. This will lessen negative feelings and allow you to focus more on what you do already have, thus enabling you to enjoy it even more. Those of us in health care know that even taking a walk or breathing without pain is a pure gift that we often take for granted. (Stop breathing for a while and such a failure to be grateful will certainly cease.)
- From your exercises in gratitude, take note of the rewarding elements in all aspects of your life. Start with the people, activities, and things that you obviously enjoy. First, see how you might take them less for granted. It may be your spouse, someone at work who makes you laugh, the quiet few moments you spend in the morning over tea or when you first get into work before others arrive. They are often simple, unnoticed moments of joy. Why let them remain that way?
- Instead of filling your evening hours watching television or sitting at the computer, develop some interactive hobbies or activities. These tend to renew us much more than passively sitting in front of a screen.
- Shift your focus from yourself to others and little service activities. Focusing only on pleasure and failing to take note of the joy that comes with reaching out will result in less ongoing happiness.
- Learn to savor life and your relationships. Whether we are looking at photos taken by a friend or relative, enjoying a note from a daughter or grandson, or gratefully recalling an experience or deed that turned a good day into one filled with fun or joy, the goal is to appreciate the many gifts we have. People who can't savor are always searching for more or what they can't have rather than fully enjoying what is already within their reach.

celebrated and reinforced. Such an approach, whether conscious or not, is already a part of the lifestyle of resilient individuals. Incorporating these approaches can help all of us build resilience. With this in mind, I close this chapter with a questionnaire (Table 10) designed to encourage consideration of how positive psychology might provide us with insights into our own behaviors, cognitions, and style of living as well as how well we are functioning at work. While the questions, in and of themselves, can enable us to entertain making changes based on new insights, it is my hope that reflecting on them will also encourage you to explore this topic further. At the end of the book you will find a selected bibliography on positive psychology. Making such reading and reflection a part of the renewal activities in our self-care protocol over the next year would be congruent with enhancing the resiliency encouraged here.

Psychologists Rick Snyder and Shane Lopez in their book *Positive Psychology: The Scientific and Practical Explorations of Human Strengths* sum it up well when they refer to positive psychology as "the study and application of that which is good in people."[17] Given this, what better area could we explore than positive psychology as part of our interest in maintaining a healthy perspective, raising our quality of life, and being more deeply involved with worthy institutions in society? Responding to the following questionnaire is a good place to begin the process of enhancing what is good in our life and our activities in those institutions which make the world better for us all.

Table 10   A Questionnaire for Self-Reflection on Personal Strengths and Virtues

Introduction

There are a number of Web sites (www.authentichappiness.org is connected with Martin Seligman's book, *Authentic Happiness*) that have online surveys on positive psychology. There are also a number of books that have developed exercises as a result of research in this field. Chief among these books are Peterson's *A Primer in Positive Psychology*, Seligman's *Authentic Happiness*, and Boldt's *Pursuing Human Strengths*. Others are also listed in the Further Reading on positive psychology provided in this book. They have been developed by the current leaders in the field and can strengthen your ability to embrace life more fully.

The questions that follow have been formulated to inspire reflection on the way we live our lives. A secondary goal is to increase your interest in reading further with an eye to deepening your own capacity and sense of fulfillment.

The overarching aim of these goals is to enhance the paradigm for self-evaluation so that the way you look at yourself is not just based on preventing, limiting, or ameliorating negative or unproductive habits, traits, or interpersonal styles. Instead, I hope the process of filling out this questionnaire will temper the more negative personal critique you might normally undertake to build self-awareness that is more balanced, potent, and accurate. The result of this? A more healthy pursuit of human strengths and virtues which, in turn, could lead to a more profound appreciation of what might contribute to a fuller life for you, your family, friends, coworkers, and those you serve or who count on you. The interpersonal circle you have with others can then be gracefully completed by your broader positive sense of self because, once again, one of the greatest gifts you can share with others is a sense of your own peace, joy, and hope, which grows from an understanding of your strengths and virtues. But you cannot share fully if you are not fully aware of these talents. It is as simple as that.

Table 10   Continued

Questions for Consideration

What persons and situations make life more joyful and meaningful for you?

How do you enhance and nurture these relationships and situations?

What do you consider to be your most important personal and professional goal?

How are you enjoying the process of achieving this goal?

What are your major strengths and virtues? (Asking family, friends, and coworkers might help you to obtain a broader and more in-depth list.)

How do you seek to apply these virtues and signature strengths in daily life?

What are your particular personal and professional/occupational talents?

How do you foster their use—especially in enhancing your ongoing relationships with others?

What motivates you to become and remain committed personally and occupationally?

What are your strategies for facing obstacles to your professional and personal growth?

In what way do your own challenges enable you to deepen and appreciate your life more fully—no matter what difficulties you may be facing?

What are some new experiences that you were open to recently that you felt were broadening for you, either at home or at work?

(continued)

Table 10 Continued

What are some recent illustrations of how you were able to recognize your own emotions and creatively employ them in an interpersonal situation?

What are some of the approaches you use to remove obstacles to your own growth?

In terms of your own strengths and virtues, what are illustrations of you at your best as a person? At work?

How are these strengths and virtues connected with your overall philosophy of what makes your life worth living?

How are you reinforcing these strengths and virtues?

What is the connection for you between exercising these strengths and:
• Developing rewarding relationships?
• Your sense of well-being as a person and at work?
• Your sense of "psychological efficacy" (the power and control you feel in life)?

How has your own resiliency on the job and at home actually been enhanced rather than diminished by very challenging encounters?

In looking over your own life, what has made you value your own life more deeply?

What ideas and beliefs do you hold concerning what makes you and others flourish as human beings?

What are some of the ways in which you ensure your autonomy personally and professionally?

Table 10   Continued

Given your personal mission/career goals in life, what is your specific plan to achieve these goals?

In what ways do you ensure your professional and personal life is balanced?

How would you describe your style of relating to those with whom you are most deeply connected?

What is it that others find most endearing about you?

Which of the following traits do you possess and value? Check each one below that relates to you. After doing that go back and add another checkmark to those that especially stand out for you—those are your *signature strengths*.

Dependable
Responsible
Open
Flexible
Welcoming
Trustworthy
Friendly
Hopeful
Understanding
Warm
Mature
Enjoyable to be with
Sympathetic
Encouraging
Energetic
A problem-solver
A conflict-resolver
Forgiving

(continued)

Table 10 Continued

Able to postpone gratification
Self-aware
Considers the greater good
Happy
Enthusiastic
Willing to listen
Strong
A lifelong learner
Considerate
Romantic
Committed
Confident
Emotionally stable
Industrious
Sociable
Empathic
Able to form close relationships
Able to set aside time for reflection, silence, and solitude
Can easily share thoughts, feelings, and hopes with others
Can monitor and regulate one's own strong emotions
Deals well with ambiguities and surprises
Is able to set priorities and follow them
Sees happiness, as opposed to pleasures, as important and knows
    what contributes to it
Sees mindfulness practices as valuable in one's own life
Has a balanced circle of friends
Able to laugh at myself
Optimistic

What are some interesting ways you can use the above talents/gifts/ strengths in unique ways in your personal life and at work?

What institutions (universities, health care facilities, religious/ community/political organizations, professional associations) are you involved in and what are the benefits both to you and the institutions themselves from your efforts?

Table 10   Continued

An article is written about you at the end of your life; what would you want included in it?

As you reflect on your life, for whom and what are you most grateful in your personal and professional life? (Please be detailed.)

What are ways that you savor good experiences in your personal and professional life? (Provide illustrations.)

What are your favorite leisure activities, and how do you ensure they are present in your schedule?

How do you increase the frequency of your contact with enjoyable/ stimulating/encouraging/inspiring/humorous friends?

Given positive psychology's philosophy of viewing your gifts and talents as clearly as your growing edges and faults, what are other questions you would need/like to ask yourself that would open up a greater appreciation of the positive aspects of your personal life and enhance the meaningfulness of the work you do?

NOTES

1. Baker, E. (2003). *Caring for ourselves: A therapist's guide to personal and professional well-being.* Washington, DC: American Psychological Association.

2. Nouwen, H. (1981). *Making all things new.* New York: Harper and Row.

3. Dowar, A. (2000). *Self-Nurture* (p. 213). New York: Penguin Group.

4. King, M. L., Jr. Source unknown.

5. (1989). An interview with Thich Nhat Hanh, Vietnamese Zen Master, *Common boundary*, Nov./Dec., 16.

6. Csikszentmihalyi, M. (2001). Foreword. In Schmuck, P. & Sheldon, K.M., *Life goals and well-being: Towards a positive psychology of human striving* (p. 5). Cambridge, MA: Hogrefe & Huber Publishing.

7. Hopkins, Anthony. (1989, July 16). The Lightning of Olivier. *The New York Times*, p. 23.

8. Williams, E., Konrad, T., Scheckler, W., Patham, D., Linzer, M., McMurray, J. et al. (2001). Understanding physicians' intentions to withdraw from practice: The role of job satisfaction, job stress, and mental and physical health. *Health Care Management Review*, 26 (1), 15.

9. Kennedy, J. F. Source unknown.

10. Quoted in: Hay, G. (1967). *The Way to Happiness* (p. 35). New York: Simon & Schuster.

11. Seligman, M. E. P. (2002). *Authentic happiness: Using the new positive psychology to realize your potential for lasting fulfillment.* New York: Free Press.

12. Seligman, M. E. P. (2002). *Authentic happiness: Using the new positive psychology to realize your potential for lasting fulfillment.* New York: Free Press.

13. Peterson, C. (2006). *A primer in positive psychology.* New York: Oxford University Press.

14. Peterson, C. (2006). *A primer in positive psychology.* New York: Oxford University Press.

15. Carr, A. (2004). *Positive Psychology: The Science of Happiness and Human Strengths.* London: Routledge.

16. Seligman, M. E. P. (2002). *Authentic happiness: Using the new positive psychology to realize your potential for lasting fulfillment.* New York: Free Press.

17. Snyder, C. R., & Lopez, S. J. (Eds.). (2002). *Handbook of positive psychology.* Oxford: Oxford University Press.

THE FIRST STEPS TOWARD
SELF-KNOWLEDGE: DEBRIEFING
YOURSELF

*It is as hard to see oneself
as to look backwards
without turning round.*

HENRY DAVID THOREAU

*The greatest pleasures come only when you are aware of yourself
and know your strengths and limitations. Your capacity to enjoy
pleasure is limited by your self-acceptance. More than anything
else, it is your openness with yourself that allows you to enjoy
life fully.*

DAVID VISCOTT, *Emotional Resilience*

If resilience is to be strengthened, if stress is to be limited, and if the quality of our personal and professional well-being is to be enhanced, then self-knowledge and enlightened behavior are not niceties; they are the first steps we all must take in life. Self-knowledge leads to personal discipline and self-management, which are essential to resilience. Psychologists call this "self-regulation." In her book on self-care, Ellen Baker writes, "*Self-regulation*, a term used in both behavioral and dynamic psychology, refers to the conscious and less conscious management of our physical and emotional impulses, drives and anxieties."[1]

Attending to how we feel as we relate with others at work and at home is not easy but essential. To manage the way we feel we need to learn how to understand and deal with anxiety, depression, and stress as well as to know how to take a step back so we can deal with intense emotions before being overwhelmed or acting on them. However, to do this we must have a sound sense of self-awareness.

It is very easy to lose our way—even from the very beginning of our journey in life or a profession—unless something or someone helps us gain perspective. Harvard psychiatrist Robert Coles, in reflecting on his early years in medical school, shares a story that aptly illustrates this:

> I was in medical school in Columbia and not enjoying it much. Kept complaining about it to my mother, and she said that what I needed was to go down and work at a [New York City] soup kitchen for Dorothy Day instead of complaining. I understood what my mother was getting at. She used to say that there are things more important than the troubles you're having, and there are people who might help you to understand that and especially help you to get some distance from your complaining and from the rather privileged position of being a medical student. The long and short of it is, I eventually went down there and met Dorothy Day.[2]

Unfortunately, this problem doesn't end with graduation, marriage, or any personal or professional milestone. Loss of perspective remains a danger all through our life and career if time isn't taken to reflect on our personal and professional lives. The following letter written by a first-year college student to her father during the middle of her second semester, delightfully points out how easy it is to lose perspective no matter how delicate and important one's work is. Prior to receiving this note, her father was totally preoccupied with her "success" in college. He was worried because she didn't do well in her first semester and was concerned she would fail out during the second semester—and take his money with her! He had forgotten, as many of us parents do, that performance in courses is only a partial measure of learning; moreover, there is much more to the total college experience than just grades.

Despite her youth, this woman knew this better than he, and so taught him an important lesson on perspective. On the front page of her note it said:

Dear Dad,

Everything is going well here at college this semester, so you can stop worrying. I am very, very happy now . . . you would love Ichabod. He is a wonderful, wonderful man and our first three months of marriage have been blissful. And more good news, Dad. The drug rehab program we are both in just told us that the twins that are due soon will not be addicted at birth.

Having read this, her father then turned the page with trepidation. On the other side of the note it said:

> Now, Dad, there actually is no Ichabod. I'm not married nor pregnant. And I haven't ever abused drugs. But I did get a "D" in chemistry, so keep things in perspective![3]

It is very easy to move through life—even the most service-oriented of lives—in such a compulsive, driven way that we feel out of control and lose perspective. When we take time out to reflect on who we are and what we are doing, we often see how burdened we have become in so many ways. In his most classic work, physician and Russian spiritual leader Anthony Bloom puts it in a way that is easy to imagine:

> There is a passage in Dickens' Pickwick Papers which is a very good description of my life and probably also of your lives. Pickwick goes to the club. He hires a cab and on the way he asks innumerable questions. Among the questions, he says, "Tell me, how is it possible that such a mean and miserable horse can drive such a big and heavy cab?" The cabbie replies, "It's not a question of the horse, sir, it's a question of the wheels,", and Mr. Pickwick says, "What do you mean?" The cabbie answers, "You see, we have a magnificent pair of wheels which are so well oiled that it is enough for the horse to stir a little for the wheels to begin to turn and then the poor horse must run for its life!"[4]

Bloom then adds by way of commentary on this: "Take the way we live most of the time. We are not the horse that pulls, we are the horse that runs away from the cab in fear of its life."[5] The bottom line is: We can count on losing perspective and deluding ourselves if time is not devoted to reflection on our thoughts, behavior, and feelings. But, as might be surmised, it often isn't easy to be honest with ourselves.

Zen master Shunryu Suzuki once cautioned his students: "When you are fooled by something else, the damage will not be so big. But when you are fooled by yourself, it is fatal."[6] In a book on the challenges of being a woman physician, the author wrote, "What's good about medicine is that there is always something to do, so you don't have time to think about your problems." Then she added: "What's bad about medicine is that there's always something to do so you don't have the time to think about your problems *enough*."[7] The same can be said of all of us today who live life fully. But knowing we should have self-knowledge is one thing; actually pursuing it with an open heart is quite another.

Real self-knowledge can even be elusive for those of us who are professionals dedicated to helping others achieve new degrees of clarity about their lives. David Brazier reflects this reality in a book advocating the use of an integration of Zen with psychotherapy when he notes:

These days . . . we are apt to seek out a therapist to . . . help us get the dragon back into its cave. Therapists of many schools will oblige in this, and we will thus be returned to what Freud called "ordinary unhappiness" and, temporarily, heave a sigh of relief, our repressions working smoothly once again. Zen, by contrast offers dragon-riding lessons, for the few who are sufficiently intrepid.[8]

And so, whether we are interested in Zen or not, given the personal psychological dangers to people in today's uncertain world, we must be among those who are "the sufficiently intrepid" with respect to our self-awareness. Several simple "self-mentoring" themes are offered here to structure the type of ongoing reflective process that is a *sine qua non* of resilience. They include:

- Understanding our unique self and being true to that self
- Embarking on a disciplined search
- Elements of clarity
- Awareness of all our agendas
- Facing failure in a productive way
- Critical thinking
- Appreciating and overcoming our own resistance to change
- Improving self-talk

UNDERSTANDING OUR UNIQUE SELF AND BEING TRUE TO THAT SELF

No matter which approach is used to understand stress—be it weighted in the direction of environment or personality—the individual is naturally always a factor. A significant turning point in therapy takes place when the individual seeking help is finally able to grasp a simple, seemingly paradoxical reality: When we truly accept our limits, the opportunity for personal growth and development is almost limitless. Before reaching this insight, energy is wasted on running away from the self, or running to another image of self. The same can be said of any of us in how we deal with our lives.

This should not be surprising since recognition of this reality is reflected in the writings of non-clinicians as well. Poets, theologians, and great men of science have joined those in the mental health field to warn people not to be unconsciously pulled into trying to be someone you are not. In the words of e.e. cummings, "To be nobody but yourself in a world which is doing its best, night and day, to make you everybody else— means to fight the hardest battle which any human being can fight, and never stop fighting."[9] Jewish theologian Martin Buber echoed this same theme from a slightly different point of view and invoked the following story:

> The Rabbi Zusya said a short time before his death, "In the world to come, I shall not be asked, "Why were you not Moses?" Instead, I shall be asked, "Why were you not Zusya?"[10]

Full self-awareness is very elusive, so we will explore ways to grasp it. If we are honest with ourselves, we will learn self-respect—an acceptance of what we have to offer and what makes us unique. Self-respect and self-awareness go hand in hand.

EMBARKING ON A DISCIPLINED
SEARCH

Self-awareness is an ongoing, dynamic undertaking that requires daily attention. When we have such a process in place we can become more attuned to the rhythm of our personality and have our "psychological fingers" on the pulse of where we are emotionally with respect to an issue, person, challenge, or the general thrust of our life's trajectory. It is based on clarity— clarity about our feelings, beliefs, actions, and reactions. The process requires energy and discipline.

To accomplish this, we need to be aware of the ebb and flow of our reactions so we can become more sensitive to the subtle inconsistencies between our affect (our experiences of sadness, depression, happiness, etc.), our cognitions (ways of thinking, perceiving, and understanding), and our actions. This provides us with a link to some of our motivations and mental agendas that lie just beyond awareness—what some would refer to as our "preconscious" or unexamined schemata or beliefs. In one sense, they are the hidden agendas that are hidden even from us. To be in a position for such an appreciation of ourselves, time must be taken to identify anything in the way we live that is incongruent: What doesn't add up?

Instead, what often happens when we do, think, or feel something that is generally out of character for us is that we fail to notice it, or dismiss it as irrelevant or excuse it. ("I was just tired, that is all.") But when we do this and do not seek to understand our actions, we will miss the normally buried treasures in our psyche that can provide clues to material that is generally not available to us for consideration. These incongruities are opportunities for self-understanding.

ELEMENTS OF CLARITY

One of the constants present when people seek help to avoid or limit the sources of stress in their lives is the temporary lack of clarity they are experiencing. In helping them to refocus, one of the goals is to help a person to clarify and discern different approaches, and ultimately to problem solve in finding solutions to inner and external stresses. To accomplish this, time must be taken to focus on the *specifics* of one's reactions. This helps the person to move through conscious (suppression) and unconscious/preconscious (repression) avoidance or forgetting. By limiting vagueness and a tendency to generalize or gloss over details and feelings, information that lies just beyond our sense of awareness becomes available. So, rather than turning away from that which is unacceptable, we face the anxieties that are produced as a price for learning more about ourselves. The benefit, of course, is greater self-knowledge and, in turn, less impulsive behavior with more personal freedom. So, rather than being limited by our blind spots in self-awareness, we can build our own self-knowledge by examining our daily interactions.

Clarity is a process by which we must be willing to look at how we may be denying, minimizing, rationalizing, or hiding things from ourselves. Although we often say that we want to see ourselves and our situation as they truly are, conflict often arises when this happens because the responsibility then falls on us to:

- Be aware of all of our own agendas—including the immature ones
- See our own defensiveness as well as our tendencies to project blame onto others
- Find appropriate levels of intimacy with those with whom we interact
- Know how to deal with anger and our unhelpful reactions to failure
- Improve our critical thinking

AWARENESS OF ALL OUR AGENDAS

Thinking that we do things for only one reason is naive. In most cases there are a number of reasons we do things—some immature, others mature. Since the ones we don't like to acknowledge tend to remain beyond our awareness, clarity calls on us to uncover and make creative efforts to embrace all of them. Through this awareness, chances will increase that the defensive motivations will atrophy while the healthy outlook is given the "psychological space" to grow and deepen. But to accomplish this goal, we must first accept that we are all defensive in some unique way. Such an admission is an excellent beginning because it doesn't put us in the position of asking: "Are we or aren't we?" Instead, it moves it out of the black-and-white situation and into the gray areas where most of us live psychologically. When we look at all the reasons why we react to situations in the way we do, we can begin to appreciate why people react to us in the way that they do. Otherwise, we will remain puzzled, consider ourselves misunderstood, and project most of the blame outward so as never to learn what the dynamics of our behavior are and how to unravel them in any given situation.

For instance, if colleagues don't like to work with us in stressful situations, it would be helpful for us to know our part in the problem so we can work on decreasing the incidence of it. For instance, once a candidate applying for a position as my assistant when I was chair of a counseling program asked me, "Do you know how the human resources department is billing the main challenge of working with you?" Surprised—after all, how could there be *any* challenge in working with me—I responded, "No, I don't." To which she replied with a shy smile, "They are billing you as a perfectionist who gives vague instructions and gets upset when they are not followed exactly." Imagine!

Impatience, anger, and other negative reactions on our part decrease our effectiveness when we are working with colleagues in a difficult situation or emergency. Blaming our reactions solely on other people's incompetence provides very limited information for improving the situation or changing our own behavior. We contribute to the problem rather than the solution.

Clarity calls on us to recognize our agendas, face our own fears, understand the games we play with others, lessen our defensiveness, develop new coping skills, and create alternative ways to deal with stressful situations. Yet to do this, we have to be honest. We also have to appreciate that this can have a positive domino effect on our life because by moving through the resistances we have, we create more opportunity for growth and change. Moreover, when we start focusing on understanding individual interactions, larger questions open up as to whether we are getting enough rest or leisure, the right balance of time alone and with good friends, and whether we are setting appropriate limits in all aspects of our life. It is important to recognize that *the self is a limited entity* which can be depleted if we don't involve ourselves seriously in a process of self-care that includes self-knowledge.

Through simple, periodic self-questioning (contained in the closing chapter of this book) we can better see our motivations, fears, and interpersonal style. The more this is accomplished, the more we will almost automatically withdraw our projections, take control of our lives and—in the process—reduce unnecessary chronic and acute stress. The problem is that, as aware adults, we take for granted that we do this as a matter of course. Unfortunately, with busy schedules, such time for structured self-awareness often isn't undertaken as often and regularly as it should be. This can develop into a real problem—especially when we are confronted with failures, as we certainly will be.

FACING FAILURE IN
A PRODUCTIVE WAY

A reality in life today is that the more you are involved, the more you are going to fail. So, you'd better be able to put failure into perspective. Failure is part and parcel of involvement. Given the many demands and the inability to be perfectly "on" all the time, failure will occur. And while this is inevitable, failure can still provide helpful information to us. For instance, it can limit future mistakes and provide better insight into how we experience life's gifts and challenges and react to them. In fact, if we look carefully at ourselves when we fall short of our own or others' goals, failure can actually teach us to:

- Recognize the dangers of pride and the need for openness
- Consider ways to avoid errors in the future
- Change factors that increase the possibility of failure
- Experiment with new interpersonal approaches
- Learn about ourselves
- Be sensitive to early warning signs of mistakes
- Consider the impact of negligence
- Uncover areas where further education, guidance, or support is required
- Appreciate unrealistic expectations
- Improve pacing in one's life
- Acknowledge professional limitations that can be improved as well as become more aware of the personal limitations in ourselves

If failure is carefully considered as an appropriate source of helpful information rather than solely as a source of self-condemnation or an impetus to blame, deny, or distort the situation, then both we and persons who cross our path will benefit immeasurably from the process of our self-examination. But to accomplish this, we must seek to be critical thinkers.

CRITICAL THINKING

Critical thinking helps us to not only grasp what is going on around us, but also to recognize our own agendas, negative emotions, attitudes, motivations, talents, and growing edges. This greater grasp of reality also stops the drain of psychological energy it takes to be defensive or protect our image. Since critical thinking is not always natural (although we may think it is) it takes discipline—a willingness to face the unpleasant, and a stamina that sustains us when we don't grow or gain insight as quickly as we'd like.

As persons with full lives requiring many decisions, the types of questions we must be willing to ask ourselves as critical thinkers are:

- Am I willing to avoid seeing things simply in black and white, and entertain ambiguity in life?
- Can I appreciate that the "answer" or "diagnosis" I have now in my life is always tentative?

- Am I able to entertain the possible as well as the probable without undue discomfort?
- Do I need to come to a quick solution or take one side of an issue because I lack the intellectual stamina that encourages an open mind to see both sides?
- Am I so uncomfortable with personal rejection, a tarnished image, or failure that I capitulate when others disagree with me?
- Am I willing to "unlearn" what I have learned that is not useful anymore and be open to new techniques and approaches?
- Do I realize the obvious and less noticeable ways that I resist change? Am I open to seeing my emotions and extreme reactions as red flags that can often indicate that I am holding on because of fear, stubbornness, or some other defensive reason?

The willingness to be a critical thinker (and face questions like the ones above) takes not only motivation but also involves an appreciation of how resistant to change most of us are much of the time without knowing it. As a result, to face these questions, we must also de facto, face our natural resistance to change as well.

APPRECIATING AND OVERCOMING OUR OWN RESISTANCE TO CHANGE

Positive change—even when we are aware that we have problems that need to be confronted—can be so elusive. As Rodman in his classic work on becoming a psychotherapist, *Keeping Hope Alive*, notes:

> Every patient stared at long enough, listened to hard enough, yields up a child arrived at from somewhere else, caught up in a confused life, trying to do the right thing, whatever that might be, and doing the wrong thing instead.[11]

But this point obviously does not only hold true for persons seeking counseling and psychotherapy. All of us need to recognize our own resistances as well. Yet, even when motivated to do so, this is sometimes easier said than done. As Thomas Merton, contemplative and author of the classic autobiographical work, *The Seven Storey Mountain*, laments:

> All day I have been uncomfortably aware of the wrong that is in me. The useless burden of pride I condemn myself to carry, and all that comes with carrying it. I know I deceive myself . . . but I cannot catch myself in the act. I do not see exactly where the deception lies.[12]

As a result, understanding as much as we can about our own hesitancy to both uncover resistances and act effectively to address those areas we need to change is essential.

The psychological concept of "resistance" has changed for psychotherapists over the years. A quick review of the evolution of this concept now would be helpful for all of us wishing to overcome our *own* barriers to personal and professional growth.

In the early years of psychology, a client's resistance to change was often looked upon as solely a *motivational* problem. When a person did not succeed in changing, the counselor might believe: "I did my job in pointing out your difficulties. In return, you didn't do yours!" The blame rested upon the one seeking change. The goal was to eliminate the resistances and get the person motivated again.

Now we recognize that when someone resists change and growth they are not purposely giving family, friends, coworkers, and counselors a hard time. Instead, they are unconsciously providing a great deal of critical information on problematic areas of their life given their personality style, history, and current situation. This material then becomes a real source of new wisdom for psychological growth, professional advancement, and spiritual insight. Though we still believe motivation is an essential key to making progress, we see that persons seeking change must also gain certain knowledge about themselves and act on it if they wish to advance. Or, in a nutshell: *Motivation or positive thinking is good, but it is obviously not enough.*

One of the primary reasons that motivation, of itself, does not automatically lead to change is that we fear that the demands involved may be too costly. We may have to see our own role in the problems we are having and do something about it. In addition, we worry about how other people will react when our behavior patterns change; the move toward health can be also surprisingly upsetting to those who are used to "the devil they know" (a person's usual defensive style). They may even feel challenged to change and they might be uncomfortable in dealing with this. Finally, seeing our own role in our problems does cause some painful reflection about the past and how much time we have wasted in behaving as we have.

But the "advantages" of staying the same are very costly; whereas the freedom and insights we uncover can greatly benefit us and those with whom we interact. Consequently, in respect to the tyranny of habit, we must take whatever measures we can to make our steps toward self-knowledge and personal or professional growth more realistic. So along with improving our own self-awareness, we need to increase our ability to detect defensiveness in our behaviors, and take what actions we can to outflank our resistances.

DETECTING RESISTANCES TO CHANGE—AND OUTFLANKING THEM!

The defense we use to export the blame for our own problems in life is called "projection." This defensive style is manifested in many obvious and quiet ways. We might deny our role in mistakes; excuse our behavior; contextualize our actions; absolve ourselves for ignoring or crossing boundaries in relationships that we shouldn't; rationalize failures; and generally remove ourselves from the equation while focusing on the negative role others have played.

We do this partly in reaction to a general tendency to go overboard when trying to take responsibility for our own role in various unpalatable events. Instead of trying to understand what part we played so we can learn from this, we move from remorse about what we've done to shame about who we are. With this movement from remorse to shame, we start to condemn ourselves, become hypercritical of our behavior, overly perfectionistic, unrealistic in our comparison with others in our life, and overly responsible with respect to the impact we did and can have.

A better approach is to recognize the need to take a step back from the event, try to frame the situation in an objective way by almost behaving as if it involved someone else, and seek to become intrigued about our role. In this way, we increase the possibility for change. At the same time, we are more likely to avoid blaming others, condemning ourselves, or getting discouraged when results don't happen immediately. Accordingly, in a spirit of mindfulness and to further reduce the resistance to change, there are several caveats I normally offer in order to outflank the blocks to growth in myself and others. They are:

1. Anything discovered does not have to be changed immediately.
2. No area should be condemned . . . just neutrally observed as if it were happening to someone else.
3. No area should be defended—no one is criticizing or attacking, just observing where the energy is being spent.

4. Observations—even disturbing ones—should be embraced as a wonderful treasure trove of information.

5. After each period of observation, the areas of concern should be written down so some record is kept of discovery.

With these provisions in mind, we can then consider the following principle with a greater sense of openness: *Where there is energy (positive or negative), there is usually a grasping or fear.* When the smoke of a strong reaction is present, the fire of desire is also usually present and we need to know what it is. Otherwise, rather than our passions being good energy, they may be the product of unexamined attachments.

They then keep us connected to views and convictions that are covering or distorting the truth rather than leading us to it. Classic signs that we are holding on include: arguing, not sharing all the information or motivations with persons with whom we discuss the event, complaining that change in certain areas is unrealistic, stonewalling persons through an icy silence or monopolizing the situation, feeling misunderstood or totally ignored, and other strong emotions or off-putting actions.

On the other hand, there are also classic signs that a person does value change, growth, and insight both professionally and personally. Some of these signs are:

- An ability to let go
- Being receptive to new lessons
- Humility

- A desire to understand one's own emotional hot-button issues
- Feeling disgusted with the endless wheel of suffering that comes from grasping and bad habits
- Curiosity, openness, nonjudgmentalism
- Valuing experience
- Recognizing the danger of attachments which prevent experiencing new gifts in life
- Being awake to the present; attentive and mindful
- Appreciative of quiet meditation
- Generous and alive
- Learning, reflecting, and applying wisdom to daily life
- Not taking oneself too seriously

In recognizing and overcoming resistances to growth and change, we are able to appreciate that the most important person in improving our situation is *ourselves*. As persons, we accept this responsibility not with a spirit of self-condemnation or overresponsibility but with a sense of intrigue about the possibility within ourselves. We can see that at times we are emotional and opinionated. We understand that blindness like this occurs because of fear and hesitation that may be partially rooted in our past but is certainly centered in a belief system that is tyrannical and often wrong. This results in a style of "self-talk" that appears to be a friend and seemingly supports us. Nevertheless, in the end it undercuts our ability to see things clearly and have solid self-esteem. Such clarity and self-esteem must be rooted in a kind of honest self-knowledge that allows us to view with equanimity our talents and gifts as well as our growing edges.

IMPROVING SELF-TALK

One of the main contributions of cognitive-behavioral psychological theory is its ability to help us better appreciate how our beliefs (schemata) and cognitions (ways of thinking, perceiving, and understanding) can impact the way we feel and behave. Ultimately, we also learn that dysfunctional ways of perceiving ourselves and the world are common and often left unchallenged. Such inattention is psychologically dangerous—especially if you are involved in stressful situations in your family life or at your workplace.

A number of years ago, in line with the work of seminal thinker Aaron Beck, psychiatrist David Burns in his popular book *Feeling Good* illustrated how people fall prey to cognitive errors that may lead to depression or an overall sense of discouragement. Perfectionistic individuals are in particular danger of such irrational thinking if they are not aware of it. Some of the well-known categories of cognitive errors include:

- *All or nothing thinking:* You see things in black-and-white categories. If your performance falls short of perfect, you see yourself as a total failure

- *Overgeneralization:* You see a single negative event as a never-ending pattern of defeat
- *Mental filter:* You pick out a single negative detail and dwell on it exclusively so that your vision of all reality becomes darkened, like the drop of ink that discolors the entire beaker of water
- *Disqualify the positive:* You reject positive experiences by insisting that they "don't count" for some reason or other. In this way you can maintain a negative belief that is contradicted by your everyday experiences
- *Emotional reasoning:* You assume that your negative emotions necessarily reflect the way things are: "I feel it, therefore it must be true."
- *"Should" statements:* You try to motivate yourself with "should" and "shouldn't." The emotional consequence is guilt. When you direct "should" statements toward others, you feel anger, frustration, and resentment
- *Personalization:* You see yourself as the cause of some negative external event which in fact you were not primarily responsible for.[13]

For me, the core of the issue here is that negative thinking is quite common. For some reason, all of us seem to give more credence to the negative than to the positive. We can hear numerous positive things but somehow allow a few negative things to discolor and disqualify the previously affirming feedback we received. Therefore, we need to (1) recognize and

acknowledge our negative thinking so we can (2) link the negative thoughts we have to the negative feeling we experience, so
(3) our negative self-talk can be replaced with a more realistic
thought or belief. In this way, we can begin to change our negative thinking so our negative beliefs can eventually be modified
as well.

We can always—and, unfortunately, frequently do—find a
negative comparison to make when we are reflecting on our
thoughts, actions, and motivations. Making negative compari-
sons between our situations and those of others is never a
problem. Maintaining perspective is the difficulty!

We may say we already know this but just can't seem to put
it into practice. When I hear this statement I think of Mark
Twain's comment: "The difference between the right word and
the almost right word is the difference between lightning and the
lightning bug." We may say we know it, but unless we can truly
recognize and short-circuit the negativity that causes insecurity
and increases defensiveness, then we really don't know it.

As Rainer Maria Rilke wrote in his classic work *Letters to
a Young Poet*:

Only someone who is ready for everything, who excludes
nothing, not even the most enigmatical, will live the relation
to another as something alive and will himself draw exhaus-
tively from his own existence. For if we think of this existence
of the individual as a larger or smaller room, it appears
evident that most people learn to know only one corner of

their room, a place by the window, a strip of floor on which they will walk up and down. Thus they have a certain security. And yet that dangerous insecurity is so much more human which drives the prisoner in Poe's stories to feel out the shapes of their horrible dungeons and not be strangers to the unspeakable terror of their abode. We, however, are not prisoners. No traps or snares are set about us, and there is nothing which should intimidate or worry us . . . We have no reason to mistrust *our* world, for it is not against us. Has it terrors, they are our terrors; has it abysses, those abysses belong to us; are dangers at hand, we must try to love them.[14]

The issue once again is: The *way* we perceive something is just as relevant as what we perceive. Only when we realize this can we see that both successes and failures can be used to increase self-understanding and self-appreciation. This is so much more life giving than seeing our successes and failures only as a constant seesaw of ups and downs. When we recognize this, how we look at or question ourselves changes dramatically, as does our overall results. And, one of the most effective ways to set the stage for having such a healthy perspective is to practice mindfulness in our lives.

NOTES

1. Baker, E. (2003). Caring for ourselves: A therapist's guide to personal and professional well-being. Washington, DC: American Psychological Association.

2. Riegle, R. (2003). Dorothy Day: Portraits by those who knew her. Maryknoll, NY: Orbis.

3. This is a very loosely adapted version of a story told by Ronald Cranfields; I was first introduced to it by Marietta Culhane, O.S.F., and I am very grateful to her for having shared it with me.

4. Bloom, A. (1970). Beginning to pray. Ramsey, NJ: Paulist Press.

5. Bloom, A. (1970). Beginning to pray. Ramsey, NJ: Paulist Press.

6. Suzuki, S. (1973). *Zen mind, beginner's mind.* New York: John Weatherhill.

7. Suzuki, S. (1973). *Zen mind, beginner's mind.* New York: John Weatherhill.

8. Brazier, D. (1995). *Zen therapy.* New York: John Wiley.

9. Cummings, E. E. (1955). Unpublished letter to a high school editor.

10. Buber, M. (1966). Way of man. New York: Lyle Stuart.

11. Rodman, F.R. (1987). *Keeping hope alive: on becoming a psychotherapist.* New York. Harper Collins.

12. Merton, T. (1988). A vow of conversation. New York: Farrar, Straus, and Giroux (p. 161).

13. Burns, D. (1980). Feeling good. New York: New American Library.

14. Rilke, R. M. (2004). Letters to a young poet. (Revised Ed.). New York: W. W. Norton & Company. (Original work published in 1954).

SOLITUDE, SILENCE, AND MINDFULNESS: CENTERING YOURSELF IN A DRIVEN WORLD

There is always music in the garden amongst the trees . . .
But your heart must be quiet to hear it.

ANONYMOUS

M any of the world's religions and ancient philosophies extol the benefits of solitude and mindfulness. But the value of silence and solitude has only recently gained traction in the West, and then only for its purely psychological worth. British psychiatrist Anthony Storr, in his classic work *On Solitude*, was one of the first to bring this subject to our awareness:

> Modern psychotherapists, including myself, have taken as their criterion of emotional maturity the capacity of the individual to make mature relationships on equal terms. With few exceptions, psychotherapists have omitted to consider the fact that the capacity to be alone is also an aspect of emotional maturity.[1]

In this volume, Storr presents Admiral Byrd as an example of someone who searched for solitude. Byrd appreciated the value of solitude as well as its offer of silence as part and parcel of his experience. Reflecting on his solo Antarctic expedition in the winter of 1934, Byrd (1938) wrote:

> Aside from the meteorological and auroral work, I had no important purposes . . . Nothing whatsoever, except one man's desire to know that kind of experience to the full, to be by himself for a while and to taste peace and quiet and solitude long enough to find out how good they really are . . . I wanted something more than just privacy in the geographical sense. I wanted to sink roots into some replenishing philosophy . . . I did take away something that I had not fully possessed before: appreciation of the sheer beauty and miracle of being alive, and a humble set of values . . . Civilization has not altered my ideas. I live more simply now, and with more peace.[2]

A more recent publication in this area is: *The Call of Solitude: Alonetime in a World of Attachment* (1997) by the psychologist Buckholz. In it, she echoes Storr's comments and the reflections of Byrd by writing: "We are born wanting and needing time and space alone to process the stimulation around us, as we also learn quickly to revel in and long for attached and related times" (p. 49). In this regard she also refers to Thoreau's Walden Pond living experiment:

> Few in our society respect the sanctity of chosen alone time. Even in a saucy book dedicated to fellow solitaires on how to

make oneself company enough, author Barbara Holland mocks Henry David Thoreau's time to himself because he was never that far from human community. The point missed, however, is that, for a while, Thoreau chose to reverse the typical priority of people over solitude, not to abandon attachments. On July 4, 1845, Thoreau made his famous autonomous move to what he hoped would be the quiet of Walden Pond in Concord, Massachusetts. "Every morning was a cheerful invitation to make my life of equal simplicity and I may say innocence, with nature herself." He went there to examine his life and to seek protection from the contamination of industrial civilization. Thoreau and his friend Ralph Waldo Emerson believed in nature's healing powers and feared social demands as impositions that took people away from their true course in life. Yet neither man was antisocial or selfish. For example, both concerned themselves with the pursuit of people's rights and were against slavery. Walden Pond stands for a successful romantic retreat from the vicissitudes of everyday life perhaps because Thoreau also responded to his needs for engagement.[3]

Psychologist Ellen Baker in her book on self-care also addresses this same theme of solitude, but with a very practical focus in mind that is certainly relevant for the rest of us as well:

Consciously building in self-time at various points in the day is a valuable self-care practice. Ziegler and Kanas (1986) suggested that [one] "set aside an hour as 'inviolate' and relax, walk, run, meditate, or otherwise get it together" (p. 180). Despite a daunting work schedule, Zeiss (1996) spoke of her goal continuing to set aside what she refers to as "sacred time" for herself and her . . . husband on the weekend.[4]

From a spiritual standpoint, long before Storr, Buckholtz, and other psychiatrists and psychologists wrote positively about silence and solitude, all the major religions pointed out the value of taking out time to retreat from activity. The same can be said of the writings of contemporary spiritual figures. For instance, Henri Nouwen, a Catholic spiritual writer (and incidentally, also a psychologist), notes in his book *The Way of the Heart* that silence and solitude are the furnace in which transformation takes place.[5]

Contemporary Buddhist author Sogyal Rinpoche in his book, *The Tibetan Book of Living and Dying*, frames such periods of silence as "meditation." He points out that slowing down the pace of our lives by ensuring we have time to stop, breathe, and see how habits and compulsions have quietly strangled us is essential. He writes:

> We are already perfectly trained . . . trained to get jealous, trained to grasp, trained to be anxious and sad and desperate and greedy, trained to react angrily to whatever provokes us. We are trained . . . to such an extent that these negative emotions rise spontaneously, without our even trying to generate them . . .

However if we devote the mind in meditation to the task of freeing itself from illusions, we will find that with time, patience, discipline, and the right training, our mind will begin to unknot itself.[6]

He then goes on to say:

The gift of learning to meditate is the greatest gift you can give yourself in this life. For it is only through meditation that you can understand the journey to discover your true nature, and so find the stability and confidence you will need to live, and die, well . . . Our lives are lived in intense and anxious struggle, in a swirl of speed and aggression, in competing, grasping, possessing, and achieving, forever burdening ourselves with extraneous activities and preoccupations. Meditation is the exact opposite.[7]

Orthodox Rabbi Aryeh Kaplan expresses a similar positive sentiment regarding meditation in his book *Meditation and Kabbalah*. He ties meditation to a number of sources, indicating the later eighteenth century and early nineteenth century as its most popular period. He also acknowledges the fact that technique is similar throughout the different world religions and points out that in Judaism there is often a lack of awareness of this tradition of meditation among practicing Jews:

With the spread of the Hasidic movement in the Eighteenth Century, a number of meditative techniques became more popular, especially those centered around the formal prayer service. This reached its zenith in the teachings of Rabbi Nachman of Breslov (1772–1810), who discusses meditation in considerable length. He developed a system that could be used by the masses, and it was primarily for this reason that Rabbi Nachman's teachings met with much harsh opposition.

One of the problems in discussing meditation, either in Hebrew or in English, is the fact that there exists only a very limited vocabulary with which to express the various "technical" terms . . .

Many people [also] express surprise that the Jewish tradition contains a formal meditative system, that, at least in its outward manifestations, does resemble some of the Eastern systems. This resemblance was first noted in Zohar, which recognized the merit of the Eastern systems, but warned against their use.

The fact that different systems resemble each other is only a reflection on the veracity of the technique, which is primarily one of spiritual liberation. The fact that other religions make use of it is of no more consequence than the fact that they also engage in prayer and worship. This does not make Jewish worship and prayer any less meaningful or unique, and the same is true of meditation. It is basically a technique for releasing oneself from the bonds of one's physical nature. Where one goes from there depends upon the system used.[8]

MINDFULNESS AND MEDITATION

Whether a person is without a proclaimed religion or is a Buddhist, Muslim, Jew, Christian, or Hindu, or has another religious or spiritual identity is not of primary concern. The point in speaking about silence and solitude, or mindfulness meditation, is that there is a benefit—especially for those of us who seek to be resilient. Mindfulness, which can be briefly defined as *awareness of present experience with acceptance,* offers us a milieu and approach for replenishing the self and maintaining perspective.

For instance, Clark Strand, a former Zen Buddhist monk who wrote the book *The Wooden Bowl* about taking out time for meditation, noted:

All I wanted in the first place was to find the simple truth about who we are and how we ought to live . . . I asked myself one question: Was there a way for people to slow down and experience themselves, their lives, and other people in the present moment . . . The only thing [meditation] requires is that you be willing to remain a beginner, that you forgo achieving any expert status . . . In other words, it requires you to maintain a spirit of lightness and friendliness with regard to what you are doing. It's nothing special, but it works."[9]

In extolling the value of being mindful, he goes on to say what he believes it offers all of us:

Perhaps you have had the experience of waking well-rested on a Saturday morning. Your mind is alert but you have not yet begun to think about the day. The sun is shining in the yard and all around you is perfectly clear morning light. That alertness sustains itself without even trying. You may not even notice it except for the feeling of being rested and ready for the day.

The experience of meditation is something like that. When you meditate you are not trying to have any particular experience. You are simply awake. After having counted your breath from one to four for several minutes, quite without having aimed at that experience, you start to feel a kind of clarity and space surrounding each number as you count. It feels a little like having enough space to think, enough room to move and breathe, or simply "be."[10]

Still, the questions remain as to how we do it. What is the cost involved in terms of time and loss of illusions about ourselves, and what benefits are possible, so we can consider whether the effort is worthwhile? By this I mean we must be able to hear our own inner voice instead of only our anxieties and the myriad fearful and negative voices that fill our outer world at home, in the classroom, at places of amusement, and that even dominate our places of worship! But in today's active life, where and when do we find such space? Furthermore, given our lack of experience with it, how will we spend this time alone in a way that renews us? We don't want to let it be just a time for moody introspection or vengeful musings about how we have been mistreated in life.

The benefits are certainly there if we approach such a place, not with a sense of duty, but as a time for returning to our self; it will become a gentle place of reassurance, reassessment, and peace if we do not add this as yet another task to be accomplished. *Time* spent in silence and solitude on a regular basis can affect us in a number of ways.

Meditation:

- Sharpens our sense of clarity about the life we are living and the choices we are making
- Enhances our attitude of simplicity
- Increases our humility and helps us avoid unnecessary arrogance by allowing time to examine the defenses and games we play (these often surface for us to see during quiet times)
- Lets us enjoy our relationship with ourselves more
- Decreases our dependence on the reinforcement of others
- Enables us to recognize our own areas of anger, entitlement, greed, and cowardice (given the opportunity to quietly review the day's activities and our reaction to them)
- Protects our own inner fire so that we can reach out without being pulled down
- Helps us to accept change and loss
- Makes us more sensitive to the compulsions in our lives
- Allows us to experience the importance of love and acceptance (which are fruits of the contemplative life) and

acknowledge the silliness and waste involved in condemning self and judging others

• Allows us to hear the gentle inner voice that reflects the spiritual sound of authenticity

• Helps us respect the need to take time to strengthen our own inner space so that we can, in turn, be more sensitive to the presence of others in our lives

In other words, taking quiet time in solitude and silence during each day can provide us with a place to breathe deeply. Yet, even when we know the true value of silence and solitude, we often run from it. For us, to value the quiet in our lives, we must know not only what these periods can do for us but also be able to really appreciate *what price they may extract from us.* Otherwise, we will just continue to speak about silence and solitude wistfully as something wonderful and never enjoy what this well of truth and support can offer us.

RECOGNIZING THE CHALLENGES OF SILENCE, SOLITUDE, AND MINDFULNESS

People always make time for what they want to do. When their schedule is full, they may get up early, stay up late, or set aside periods during the day, even if it turns out to limit their lunch break. So, why would we not want to set aside time for quiet periods if we feel they really have so many benefits?

Silence speaks eloquently in solitude; while listening quietly to our hearts allows us to walk unprotected and unguarded with the Truth in our inner "garden." This time of quiet listening may also present us with a challenge: It may bring us to a place of loneliness and vulnerability, open us to a new recognition of hidden lies. So, although the process of taking time away from our daily activities is essential and good, there are elements with which we will find it difficult to deal once we embrace silence and solitude. We should know about this challenging reality so that the unconscious hesitancy to take quiet time doesn't surprise us and totally undermine our efforts to seek solitude. Time away for reflection is too valuable to lose because of ignorance or hidden anxiety.

Our natural tendency is to actively avoid silence and time alone. Distracting and amusing ourselves with activities is a much more common practice than being involved on a regular basis in the process of reflection. It confronts us with the awkward way we often live out our days. Likewise, in silence, we are reminded of our mortality. Consequently, talking about mindfulness is a lot easier than meditating. Thus, when we seek to establish a life of reflection or further pursue knowledge of the self, we must realize that the process won't go as smoothly as we'd like. A road sign at the beginning of a highway construction site outside of Washington, DC warns:

BE PREPARED TO BE FRUSTRATED!

As we travel along the road to meditation and mindfulness, the same advice is often appropriate. The difficult experiences we encounter during periods of solitude need not be considered negative even if we initially feel that way. If we neither avoid nor run away from them, we can learn to understand and appreciate the constructive moments of our periods of loneliness, vulnerability, and discovery.

For instance, a number of years ago, as I was walking down a winding Virginia road with my mentor, I shared with him an unusual experience I had during my quiet time. I said to him, "My life is basically quite good. I don't feel deprived or needy. Instead, most of the time I feel grateful and challenged. However, lately in my quiet time of reflection, I have felt a sense of wistful loneliness, like something was missing. I felt a light ache of emptiness passing through my stomach . . . that something real, important and basic was missing, and I deeply yearned for it—whatever this 'it' was."

His response surprised me. He did not brush off my experience as of no consequence, advise that it would pass shortly, or tell me how to combat it. Instead he said, "That's good. The loneliness that you describe is meant to remind you that your heart will not be ultimately satisfied by anyone or anything now in this life. Your loneliness also reminds you that even though you may distract yourself with many things and people—even lovely ones—your sense of being at home can only be given by something deeper, greater. And so, the loneliness will allow you to enjoy people, things, and life in general *in their proper perspective*. As a result, you can enjoy the people and gifts in life, but they will not become idols for you because your loneliness will teach you. Then, rather than being tempted to 'set up tents' prematurely when you have wonderful experiences or relationships, you will have the freedom to enjoy them without being captured and controlled by your desire for them. Therefore, the loneliness will keep your heart open, aware; your journey will continue with a sense of passion and expectancy. That is, if you let it and don't try to avoid or 'medicate' such initially troubling feelings with activities, distractions, or work."

Andrew Harvey, in his famous book *A Journey in Ladakh*, approaches this feeling from a Buddhist perspective by offering a response he received from someone with whom he shared a similar situation:

> As we parted, he hugged me and said, "You smile a great deal. And you listen well, but I see that somewhere you are sad. I see nothing has satisfied you . . . "
>
> I started to protest.
>
> "No," he said, "nothing has satisfied you, not your work, not your friendships, not all your learning and traveling. And that is good. You are ready to learn something new. Your sadness has made you empty; your sadness has made you open!"[11]

A PSYCHOLOGICAL VACUUM

As well as opening us to loneliness and vulnerability, silence and solitude can form a psychological vacuum into which many feelings, memories and awarenesses (which lie just below the surface in the preconscious) may be encouraged to surface. At such times as these, we are being called in reflection to face the truths about ourselves that for some unconscious reason we may have put aside, denied, or diminished.

Having such truths surface is not terrible, of course, especially if we remember that many of these insights will actually be helpful rather than harmful. The only "damage" is that which will be suffered by the false image of ourselves that we have created because we haven't been willing to trust in our own inherent value. So by spending time in silence and solitude, we will be able to see the extent to which our self-worth has, to this point, been built upon a foundation of sand. We will come to recognize that our sense of self-worth is dependent in an exaggerated way on praise by others, positive experiences we have (including ones in prayer and meditation), and a list of other past achievements. Though unpleasant, finding out this truth is still life-giving. Such an epiphany allows us to rediscover a sense of self and worth grounded in true self-respect. We then can come to understand that real self-respect is based on a deep, concrete trust in the inherent spiritual value of being a mindful person rather than on specific accomplishments or the reception of kudos from others.

Arriving at this point of insight is not a magical process. The desire to be a person who is solidly aware of self-worth no matter what others say or do, no matter what mistakes or shameful things we might do, cannot thrive as just a wishful thought.

It has to be welcomed and passionately sought in silence and solitude, that place in which a strong and healthy attitude toward *all* of life is formed.

Once we consider taking out the time to sit in silence and solitude or are involved in mindfulness meditation in a group, we may then come up with another set of objections. The *first objection* may be: "When I quiet down and try to enjoy the silence, all I do is hear the noise of my thoughts and worries. So I know I'm not made for meditation or reflection." This is a typical objection of beginners. It needs to be handled; otherwise, we will quit after a couple of minutes, no matter how many times we try.

The reality is that most of us hear noise in our minds all day long. When we sit in silence the first important bit of information we learn is just how preoccupied we are with so many things. Knowing this is helpful because it:

- Helps us let the static expend itself (given a chance, after a while, our mind calms down)
- Gives us some indication of the type of worries we have about which we feel helpless or anxious (we get a chance to hear what we are continually thinking)
- Prepares us to empty our minds so we can breathe deeply, relax, and experience "the now" rather than always being caught in the past or preoccupied with the future

So, expecting the noise and letting it move through us are two ways we can meet the objection that we are not suited or able to quietly reflect or meditate. The reality we must remember is: Many people of all personality types have found meditation wonderfully helpful. It is not just for a certain type of person.

A *second objection* might be: "Meditation or reflection is too hard and alien. I'm not a yogi and have found meditation or even quiet prayer uncomfortable." The response to this is simple:

- Find a quiet place (alone if possible)
- Sit up straight
- Close your eyes or keep them slightly open looking a few feet in front of you
- Count slow, naturally exhaled breaths from one to four and repeat the process
- Relax and let stray thoughts move through you like a slow-moving train, observe them objectively, then let them go
- Experience living in the now

A *third objection* often comes in the form of a question: "What will this time do for me? I'm a busy person and time is too precious for me to deal with impractical exercises." There are many responses to this. For our purposes here—namely, the desire to change, grow, and be more resilient—the following are especially relevant:

- When we are quiet we are able to experience all of the pulls, anxieties, and conditioned responses we have going on all day but may fail to notice. So, at the very least, it informs us of the nature of the blocks we put up that thwart our ability to feel at ease, flexible, open, and ready to change when necessary.

- Not only will we be able to see what absorbs us, but how without realizing it these things have become our most important reference point or center of psychological or spiritual gravity.

- Once we have this information we can take note of it and reflect on it mentally, in journaling, or with a mentor during other periods outside of the quiet time.

- Also, the peaceful times when we sit and reflect physically stop us from running, running, running, without taking a breath, and so we experience what it means to be alive and, in the process, ask ourselves if where we are is where we want to focus our lives.

If it sounds like I'm putting great emphasis on quiet time, I am. I have found if we give some space to ourselves and try not to judge ourselves and others harshly, avoid panicking, or try to immediately solve a problem, but instead calm ourselves down, we will learn not to jump to quick conclusions; our usual ways of doing business (our programming) will not take over. This will allow our habits to loosen their hold on us so we can see life—including ourselves—differently.

When people do express their gratitude for my recommendation that they take at least two minutes a day for quiet reflection first thing in the morning, they often report extending it to twenty minutes. Then they try to find another ten minutes during the day to reconnect with the experience and find another few minutes in the evening to become tranquil, give closure, and release the day before they go to sleep.

In guiding others toward using meditation as a building block to enable change, one of the other things I also notice is that it loosens people up throughout their whole day—not just during the reflection period. The more we allow our thoughts to inform, rather than frighten, depress, or anger us, the less we are grasped by our sometimes rigid thinking and interpretations. We are not in a vise but are instead free to use our power of observation, analysis, and curiosity to help us learn valuable lessons about life. Meditation not only frees us to be open during the period of reflection, it also produces an attitude that makes us less defensive and more intrigued when we stumble as well as when we triumph. It can positively contaminate our day!

LISTENING AND REFLECTION: CORNERSTONES OF MINDFULNESS

Listening to the people around us and opening ourselves to what we hear coming from within us may cause us some shame and emotional pain at first, if we are really honest. However, just as we should not turn our backs on others who would help us see the truth, we must also have the patience and fortitude to "just sit" and be quiet when all that comes from within rises to the surface. As Achaan Chah advises:

> Just go into the room and put one chair in the center. Take the one seat in the center of the room, open the doors and windows, and see who comes to visit. You will witness all kinds of scenes and actors, all kinds of temptations and stories, everything imaginable. Your only job is to stay in your seat. You will see it all arise and pass, and out of this wisdom and understanding will come.[12]

By having a listening spirit, we recognize that we must face things directly. The American Buddhist nun Pema Chodron addresses this issue in her book *When Things Fall Apart.* She writes:

> The trick is to keep exploring and not bail out, even when we find out something is not what we thought . . . [a] sign of health is that we don't become undone by fear and trembling, but we take it as a message that it's time to stop struggling and look directly at what's threatening us.[13]

Being as open as we can in both meditation and in our relationships can teach us a great deal about ourselves if we really *listen*—a very important word to the people and world around us. By opening ourselves up, despite the pain that may be associated with it, possibilities will fill and surround us and sometimes even come kicking, scratching, or begging at our door.

And so, what we are speaking about here in the effort to be a true listener to whatever provides greater awareness and inner strength is not something to be taken lightly. Put another way: The interior life, then, is not an imaginary or psychotic world. It is not a place to run to so we can pout, brood, fantasize revenge, or ruminate over things as a way to mentally beat ourselves up. Instead, it is a place of self-knowledge, self-nurturance, challenge, and peace. It is a place that will not only be our strength but also a place of strength that we can offer to others. When our interior life is strong, our attitude toward others is gentle. When our inner life feels nourished, our hearts can be open to others' pain.

In a reflection on our time together, one person with whom I journeyed said: "And what will I leave behind from our relationship: my 'stuckness,' my unconsciousness, my shame and guilt, my repressed pain, resentment, and depression. And what will I take with me? What will be awakened through the gift of our relationship? My playfulness, my love of life, my sense of wonder, my gratitude, my openness, and my wholeness."

Unfortunately, though, our inner life is often infected by some of the negative "atmosphere" of our upbringing. For instance, Maxim Gorky in his autobiography wrote: "Grandfather's house was filled with a choking fog of mutual hostility. It poisoned the grown-ups and even infected the children."[14]

Our response to such influences is to build a persona inside that is filled with fear, hesitancy, prickliness, and anger—not a very gentle place for us to center ourselves and greet life or form an attitude to welcome others.

Moreover, when our inner life is narrow and distorted, our understanding, appreciation, and grasp of life also suffer dramatically. Carl Jung, the famous Swiss psychiatrist, put it in these terms:

> People become neurotic when they content themselves with inadequate or wrong answers to the question of life. They seek position, marriage, reputation, outward success or money, and remain unhappy and neurotic even when they have attained what they were seeking. Such people are usually confined within too narrow a spiritual horizon . . . If they are enabled to develop more spacious personalities, the neurosis generally disappears.[15]

What he is speaking about here is the inner life we all long for where we find a deep well within ourselves, where we will remain calm and pure no matter how stormy, violent, or polluted the interpersonal "weather" around us becomes. The inner life is important because it impacts every aspect of our living since we interpret all aspects of life through this inner sense of self. For instance, one person who was sexually abused at a very young age said at the end of therapy that, early in her life, transitions seemed abrupt, fearful, and everything seemed worse after them. "Now that I am in a different place in my heart," she said, "transitions are to be reached out to with wonder and awe."

The state of our interior life *does* make a difference to others. When we have a gentle, healthy, and strong inner life, we are part of the healing stillness in the world which offers places of hope to all who suffer and yearn for justice, solace, and encouragement. But if we, like so many others, do not feel at home within ourselves, and by ourselves, we will then add to the sense in the world that nowhere is there a safe and good place.

This is a very dangerous situation not only for us but also for the young who follow and try to model themselves after us. Ten years ago one pediatrician noted to me that she saw the light go out in the eyes of many fifth and sixth graders—now she sees this same sad shroud over their spontaneity in the second and third grades.

So, we need to build our inner life piece by piece today with sensitivity to our need for patience and perseverance, spiritual sanity, and self-knowledge. Not just for us do we do this but also for our family, friends, and coworkers.

But being a listening-reflective person does require some sense of a structured intention rather than just motivation and goodwill. In addition to structured time dedicated to silence and solitude for mindfulness meditation in which there is no agenda, informal reflection also involves the following elements:

1. Finding time to reflect
2. Selecting meaningful events in our day and life to reflect upon

3. Entering those events by reliving them in our minds
4. Openness to learn what we can from our desires, goals, and philosophy of life
5. Enlivening the learning through action

Such a *Structured Listening-Reflective Exercise* might involve several key elements and actions. Included among them are:

1. *Time*: A little time is needed to reflect on the day's events. If we rush through life without thought, it will catch up with us. Comments like, "Where did the time go?" indicate that we are letting others or events take over our days. When our life is passing like a blur it doesn't mean we live very *active* lives. What it does show is that we are leading *busy* lives. The difference between active and busy is the former includes reflection and is directed, whereas the busy life feels out of control and does not seem purposeful or meaningful.

2. *Select*: To make our reflection useful and not just a time to preoccupy ourselves, worry, or let our minds wander, we should pick out *specific* events or interactions during the day that caused a significant reaction.

3. *Enter*: Then we should put ourselves back into the events so we can relive them. This time, as we experience the encounter or event, we can observe our reactions, note them, and see what themes or understanding we can glean. (Remember, don't *blame* others or yourself, just neutrally observe and seek to analyze.)

4. *Learn*: Given what we understand and what our core beliefs (psychological or spiritual) are about life, what did we learn from this reflection? Often when we have values, we can see how we followed those values or ignored them.

5. *Action*: Finally, learning is only important when it changes the way we live. How we will act on our new learning is essential. And it can't be action that is immature such as making the vow *"I'll never trust him again!"* when you feel a person has let you down. Instead, using the example just cited, try to see what it was about this interaction that led you to be naive and put more trust in a certain person than he or she deserved. So, in other words, action must be based on insight that we have about our *own* behavior, beliefs, and thoughts. Otherwise, the results will be just a sophisticated form of pouting, projecting, and avoiding opportunities for self-understanding.

When we become true mindful listeners, we practice being people who recognize that there are many voices calling to us of which we are not aware. The sources of these voices may be good in their own way and can include: the desire to succeed, be well off financially, admired, spectacularly effective, or loved. The sources can be career, family upbringing, society, the health care system, politics, or culture. The important thing when we make daily decisions as well as the ones which impact us in the long run is to know which one(s) are primary at any given time so we can more clearly decide what we wish to do in any given situation. One of the positive outcomes of a strong "inner life" is an improved level of self-awareness. However, beyond this, for all of us, mindfulness can improve our overall quality of life and, in turn, benefit those with whom we interact each day.

MINDFULNESS AND WELL-BEING WHEN CONFRONTED WITH THE NEEDS OF OTHERS

As David Brazier points out in his book *Zen Therapy*:

Mindfulness is an attempt to regain contact with the flow of experience.

Mindfulness is both radical introspection and direct connection with the phenomenal world. It is not simply inward looking. It is more a matter of being fully present in each step of life. . . . Simple degrees of mindfulness are immensely valuable, indeed essential at all levels of personal growth.[16]

Kornfield poetically indicates further that through mindfulness:

We allow ourselves the space of kindness. There is beauty in the ordinary. We invite the heart to sit on the front porch and experience from a place of rest the inevitable comings and goings of emotions and events, the struggles and successes of the world.[17]

MINDFULNESS CAN BE LEARNED

Mindfulness meditation practices were given a major advance with the onset of Jon Kabat-Zinn's work. His development of Mindfulness-Based Stress Reduction (MBSR) at the University of Massachusetts Medical Center's Stress Reduction Clinic demonstrated both in his intensive training and his books (see selected bibliography) that *mindfulness can be learned.*

During a workshop sponsored by Harvard Medical School on "Mindfulness and Psychotherapy" a psychiatrist whispered a question to me during one of the breaks. He asked: "Everyone here seems to have a mindfulness practice? Do you?" Implicit in his question was, "How does one begin developing such a practice? It seems so overwhelming and elusive."

We have already touched on some basic answers to this very question and concern about the seeming elusiveness of mindfulness. Let's recap.

• Take at least a few minutes in silence and solitude each morning to center yourself. Do this by selecting a quiet place, sitting up straight, and simply counting your breaths from one to four while allowing whatever thoughts that arise to pass through you without suppressing or entertaining them.

• Ensure you have breaks between activities, groups, or meetings to quiet and separate yourself from what you have experienced so you can decontaminate yourself from the stressful elements of intensive encounters you have with others.

- Be faithful to the self-care protocol you have developed (presented in the chapter, "Navigating Life's Rough Waters: Riding the Crest of Chronic and Acute Stress" earlier in this book).
- Ensure you take a brief walk at least once during the day.
- Provide time for the *Structured Listening-Reflective Exercise* previously described in this chapter.
- Outline and practice the four basic strategies to help stay centered that were listed above.
- Begin each day and task by taking a few breaths to center yourself.
- Allow a little extra time to get to appointments so you don't arrive harried.
- Provide some breaks during the day and week so you feel refreshed rather than overwhelmed or exhausted.
- Stay in touch with your feelings so you know when you need a little time away (coffee/tea break, short walk outside the house or office).
- And finally—and possibly of greatest import with respect to reinforcing all of the above steps—read, reflect upon, and practice exercises and principles you feel are appropriate that are included in the books from the selected bibliography on mindfulness.

As Charles Germer aptly recognizes:

> Any exercise that alerts us to the present moment with accep-
> tance cultivates mindfulness. Examples are directing attention
> to one's breathing, listening to ambient sounds in the envi-
> ronment, paying attention to our posture at a given moment,
> labeling feelings, and so forth. The opportunities are
> endless.[18]

The question in response to the suggestion "Be present"
may be, "Am I not doing that now?" The response that this
chapter has attempted to offer to this question is: Yes, but qual-
itatively you can live in a more mindful way with a bit more
attention, some structure, and a little more awareness of what
experienced practitioners have to teach us. As Andrew Weiss
notes in his book *Beginning Mindfulness*:

> Meditation is not just something you do on a cushion or
> chair. Anything you do is an occasion to engage yourself
> mindfully in the present moment . . . Ultimately, the path of
> mindfulness will lead you to a place within yourself where
> you may encounter the world without ideas or preconcep-
> tions, where you can disengage from your habitual narrative
> and free yourself from mental constructs [which] . . . gives us
> a way through suffering to joy.[19]

Psychiatrist Arthur Deikmann in reflecting on the life and
teachings of Shunryu Suzuki (whose books on mindfulness—
Zen Mind, Beginner's Mind and *Not Always So*—are classics) said,

"Where he is, is where I want to be ... in that place of sanity."[20]
To be in such a place ourselves requires attention, time, desire,
and some guidance.

By way of closing this chapter, I offer here several quotes
from three of the books on mindfulness that you will find listed
at the end of this book: Andrew Weiss' *Beginning Mindfulness*
(2004), Bhante Henepola Gunaratana's *Mindfulness* (2002), and
the nationally acclaimed book by Jon Kabat-Zinn, *Wherever You
Go There You Are: Mindfulness Meditation in Everyday Life* (1994). The
first two authors provide simple advice on the process of mindfulness and I believe reinforce well that mindfulness can indeed
be learned. They provide some simple building blocks on
mindfulness that can be used immediately. Additional readings
in this area, prepared by experienced guides, are listed in the
selected bibliography at the end of this book. The final quote
from Jon Kabat-Zinn is a call to wake up now; it is, to my mind,
one of the most simple, yet compelling statements on the importance of living a mindful life I have ever read. I leave you with
several quotes. All of them I hope will whet your appetite to
read more and to begin practicing and improving your own
sense of mindfulness in daily life.

Andrew Weiss

Mindful meditation ... is about waking up. We spend most
of our lives caught up in the conceptual knowledge we have
acquired, and in our concepts of who we are, or what our lives

mean, or what a tree is or what a boulder is, and so on and on. This layer of concept sits between us and the reality of the present moment . . . To allow this layer to drop away we first have to be able to stop.[21]

Bhante Henepola Gunaratana

The process of meditation is extremely delicate, and the result depends absolutely on the state of mind of the meditator. The following attitudes are essential to success in practice . . .

1. *Don't expect anything.* Just sit back and see what happens.
2. *Don't strain.* Don't force anything or make grand, exaggerated efforts . . .
3. *Don't rush.* There's no hurry, so take your time.
4. *Don't cling to anything, and don't reject anything.* Let come what comes . . . Don't fight with what you experience, just observe it all mindfully.
5. *Let go.* Learn to flow with all the changes that come up . . .
6. *Accept everything that arises.* Accept your feelings, even the ones you wish you didn't have . . .
7. *Be gentle with yourself* . . . You may not be perfect but you are all you've got to work with . . .
8. *Investigate yourself.* Question everything . . . The entire practice hinges upon this desire to be awake to the truth.

9. *View all problems as challenges.* Look upon negatives that arise as opportunities to learn and grow . . .

10. *Don't ponder.* You don't need to figure everything out. Discursive thinking won't free you from the trap. In meditation, the mind is purified naturally by mindfulness, by wordless bare attention.

11. *Don't dwell upon contrasts.* Differences do exist between people, but dwelling upon them is a dangerous process. Unless carefully handled, this leads directly to egotism.[22]

Jon Kabat-Zinn

If what happens now does influence what happens next, then doesn't it make sense to look around a bit from time to time so that you are more in touch with what is happening now, so that you can take your inner and outer bearings and perceive with clarity the path that you are actually on and the direction in which you are going? If you do so, maybe you will be in a better position to chart a course for yourself that is truer to your inner being—a soul path, a path with heart, your path with a capital P. If not, the sheer momentum of your unconsciousness in this moment just colors the next moment. The days, months, and years quickly go by unnoticed, unused, unappreciated.

It is all too easy to remain on something of a fog-enshrouded, slippery slope right into our graves; or, in the fog-dispelling clarity which on occasion precedes the moment of death, to wake up and realize that what we had thought all those years about how life was to be lived and what was important were at best unexamined half-truths based on fear or ignorance, only our own life-limiting ideas, and not the truth or the way our life had to be at all.

No one else can do this job of waking up for us, although our family and friends do sometimes try desperately to get through to us, to help us see more clearly or break out of our own blindnesses. But waking up is ultimately something that each one of us can only do for ourselves. When it comes down to it, wherever *you* go, there *you* are. It's *your* life that is unfolding.[23]

NOTES

1. Storr, A. (1988). *On solitude.* New York: Bantam Dell.

2. Storr, A. (1988). *On solitude.* New York: Bantam Dell.

3. Buckholz, E. (1997). *The call of solitude: Alonetime in a world of attachment.* New York: Simon & Schuster.

4. Baker, E. (2003). *Caring for ourselves: A therapist's guide to personal and professional well-being.* Washington, DC: American Psychological Association.

5. Nouwen, H. (1991). *The way of the heart: The spirituality of the desert fathers and mothers.* New York: HarperOne.

6. Rinpoche, S. (1992). *The Tibetan book of living and dying.* New York: HarperCollins.

7. Rinpoche, S. (1992). *The Tibetan book of living and dying.* New York: HarperCollins.

8. Kaplan, A. (1982). *Meditation and kabbalah.* York Beach, ME: Samuel Weiser.

9. Strand, C. (1988). *The wooden bowl.* New York: Hyperion.

10. Strand, C. (1988). *The wooden bowl.* New York: Hyperion.

11. Harvey, A. (2000). *A journey in ladakh: Encounters with Buddhism.* New York: Mariner Books.

12. Kornfield, J. (1993). *A path with a heart* (p. 31). New York: Bantam Dell.

13. Chodron, P. (1997). *When things fall apart.* Boston: Shambhala Publications.

14. Gorky, M. (1996). *Gorky: My childhood.* London: Penguin.

15. Jung, C. Source unknown.

16. Brazier, D. (1995). *Zen therapy.* New York: John Wiley & Sons.

17. Kornfield, J. (1993). *After the ecstasy, The laundry* (p. 208). New York: Bantam Dell.

18. Germer, C., Siegel, R., & Fulton, P. (Eds.) (2005). *Mindfulness and psychotherapy.* New York: Guilford Press.

19. Weiss, A. (2004). *Beginning mindfulness: Learning the way of awareness.* Novato, CA: New World Library.

20. Quoted in:Chadwick, D. (1999). *The crooked cucumber* (p. 313). New York: Bantam Dell.

21. Weiss, A. (2004). *Beginning mindfulness: Learning the way of awareness.* Novato, CA: New World Library.

22. Gunaratana, B. (2002). *Mindfulness in plain English.* Somerville, MA: Wisdom Publications.

23. Kabat-Zinn, J. (1994). *Wherever you go there you are: Mindfulness meditation in everyday life.* New York: Hyperion.

THE SIMPLE CARE OF A HOPEFUL
HEART: A BRIEF EPILOGUE

*Resilience is commonly thought of as "bouncing back," like a
spring, to our precrisis shape or norm. A more apt metaphor for
resilience might be "bouncing forward," rebounding and
reorganizing adaptively to fit new challenges or changed conditions.
For instance, with a major loss—a job, a home, or a life
partner—we must forge a new pathway. When events of great
magnitude occur, such as a natural disaster like a hurricane, we
may not be able to return to "normal" life as we knew it. In
rebuilding our lives, we must construct new patterns and
recalibrate "normal" settings to meet unanticipated challenges.
With major catastrophic events, we may have to question old
assumptions and grapple with a fundamentally altered conception
of ourselves in relation to others in our shared world.*[1]

FROMA WALSH, *Strengthening Family Resilience*

The "range of resilience" is different for each person based
on a unique combination of hereditary, psychological,
and sociological factors. However, if we are truly interested in
resilience, the goal is to find ways to maximize our own range
of resilience, and in so doing, improve our quality of life and the
ability to continually renew ourselves. It has been emphasized
throughout this book that there are key elements that can
help us to maintain resilience: minimizing the effects of stress;

cultivating an inner life; and developing new skills and actions that can help us thrive rather than merely survive.

In *Bounce*, these broad areas were addressed by viewing chronic and acute stress; developing a tailored self-care program/ protocol; embarking on a disciplined self-awareness process that includes discovering and enhancing our own signature strengths; and being aware of the powerful renewing possibilities of solitude, silence, and mindfulness.

The primary message has been that moving to the higher end of our own resilience range is in our grasp; it can be learned. But following through on this information, on "having a life" no matter what the odds, is not always easy.

And so, this information and the exercises provided must lead us to *practice, practice, practice*. In this way, the simple points made can become integrated into our own unique lifestyle. That is also why I close this book with an exercise in strengthening the inner life by creating and reflecting upon *our own* resilience profile. (See Appendix A.) It is also why the section "Further Reading" appears: By revisiting the principles of resilience from different vantage points and in seeing how others thrived against great odds we can recognize how greater resilience can become a reality for us as well.

Once again: It is not the amount of darkness in the world that matters. It is not even the amount of darkness in ourselves that matters. It is how we stand in that darkness that makes all the difference in how we lead our lives in ways that positively impact others as well as ourselves. For as Carl Frederick Beuchner once said, "They may forget what you said but they will never forget how you made them feel."[2]

Understanding resilience and practicing exercises that lead to self-knowledge and mindfulness can deepen our resources and make a difference in the world. In the end, it is the difference between having a sense of the world that is dark and one that is enhanced by a hopeful heart. Now more than ever, the world very much needs the healing presence of resilient people—especially those who have been through trials themselves. It is essential to spend the time, energy, and effort to prepare for, learn from, and meet the challenges we face in the healthiest way possible. And it is to these worthy goals and to encourage those who would step toward them that this book is dedicated.

NOTES

1. Walsh, F. (2006). *Strengthening family resilience* (2nd ed.). New York: Guilford Press.

2. Suzuki, S. (2001). In D. Chadwick (Ed.). *To shine one corner of the world* (p. vii). New York: Broadway Books.

CREATING AND REFLECTING UPON YOUR OWN STRESS-RESILIENCE PROFILE: AN EXERCISE IN STRENGTHENING YOUR INNER LIFE

N ow that you have had a chance to read this book, take some time by yourself to reflect on how it relates to you. To facilitate this process, a *Stress-Resilience Self-Awareness Profile Questionnaire* is provided, followed by *An Individual Reflection Guide* with some ideas on how to think about your responses. This questionnaire is designed to enable you to review your attitudes and practices on self-care, personal stress, mindfulness, positive psychology, and self-awareness as they affect your own resiliency.

Every person has a personal resiliency range. The essential point in this book is that we must do all we can to *maximize our own range* through self-knowledge and self-care. Below are some simple instructions to set the stage; then the questionnaire is provided. Naturally, in responding to the questions, each person's pace will be different. The one constant is that the more honest, energetic, and detached you can be, the more helpful your answers will prove to be.

STRESS-RESILIENCE SELF-AWARENESS QUESTIONNAIRE

Instructions: Find a quiet, comfortable, and private place. Read each question and respond on a separate sheet of paper by writing the first thing that comes to mind. Once you have completed a page, do not turn back to it or refer to it when working on the other pages. Work as quickly as you can without setting a pace that is too stressful.

1. Do you find yourself denying that you have personal and professional stresses in your life? Why do you think you deny or minimize these stresses? What are the most common distortions that you are prone to make when viewing the causes and manifestations of stress in your life?
2. At this point what are the most realistic and helpful steps you can take to prevent, limit, and learn from stress?
3. What are the ways you have heard that are excellent approaches to reducing stress and improving self-care but you feel are unrealistic in your case? What would it take to make them realistic? ("A miracle!" is not an acceptable answer.)

4. When you think of the terms "burnout," and "traumatic stress" what do you think of in terms of your own life?

5. What are the issues that make you most anxious? What are the ones you deal with the best?

6. What are the types of situations or interactions from the past which still haunt you?

7. Given the realistic demands of work and family, what would it take to balance these two areas in your life a bit more? (List only those steps which can be realistically taken by you within the next two to three years.)

8. In your own case, what helps you to fall prey to the common masochistic tenet: "The only worthy person is the one involved enough to be on the edge of burnout or physical fatigue"?

9. In what ways did your education and modeling by others in your family and at work inadvertently teach you that taking care of yourself is a sign of weakness and an unhealthy lifestyle is the price of being a good employee or family member?

10. What are the "bad habits" of the people you observe in your family or work profession that you don't want to emulate? How are you seeking to embrace the wonder, passion, and intense involvement in family life and work?

11. When you are under a great deal of stress what fantasies do you have? What do you think are healthy fantasies that you should act upon someday? What are the unhealthy

ones which, if acted upon, would cause you and others harm?

12. What elements that are in your self-care protocol now have been the most beneficial for you? What are the least?

13. What do you struggle with most in your efforts to take care of yourself?

14. How would people describe your attitudes toward work?

15. What should be included in your list of personal doubts and insecurities that most people would be surprised to know about you?

16. In mindfulness, focusing on the person or situation that is before you is essential; what do you find are the main sources of external distraction and inner preoccupation that prevent you from doing this?

17. How does your personality both positively and negatively impact on your family, friends, or coworkers?

18. When under extreme stress, what is the style of interacting with others and handling the situation that you would most like to change? What steps are necessary to produce such a change?

19. What would you include in your list of motivations for reading this book?

20. Have the primacy of certain motivations in your work (altruism, monetary rewards, security, achievement, personal/professional growth) changed for you over time? If

so, how? Why do you think this is so? If this is problematic in some way, what might you do about it? For those beneficial changes in priorities, how are you ensuring that they remain in focus for you?

21. What are the most awkward subjects for you to discuss with regards to your emotional and physical well-being?

22. Where do you feel your narcissism/building up your own ego comes into play in your role at work or in the family?

23. What would be included in a list of what you like best about the role you have at work? What would be on the list of what you like least?

24. What is most surprising to you about the professional life you now have?

25. What are the most frustrating aspects in the work arena? Your personal life?

26. If you have ever considered changing jobs or leaving the field you are now in, what are the reasons for this?

27. When you think of the job or profession you are now in, how would you describe it for someone thinking of entering the field now? Suppose someone asked you how you thought it would be different in five years, what would you say?

28. What are the most important self-care procedures you have put into place in the past five years? What has been their impact on you? What ways would you now like to modify your plan?

29. Given your own personality style, what types of persons do you find most challenging? What types of colleagues, subordinates, and supervisors are able to easily elicit an emotional reaction from you? Given this, what ways have you found to most effectively interact with them? (Praying for their early happy death is not a sufficient response.)

30. How would you describe the seemingly beneficial and adverse impact your professional/work life have had on your personal life, and vice versa?

31. What are the five mistakes that you fear most in your work?

32. What stressors do you think you can lessen in your life by giving them some attention? What stressors do you feel powerless to alter?

33. How would you describe the differences in the sources of stress and the approaches to self-care between those for you and those for other jobs or professions?

34. How self-aware do you feel you are? On what do you base this conclusion? What would help you gain greater self-awareness?

35. If you were to divide your personal needs for happiness into "necessary" and "desirable," what would be on each list? What would be on similar lists (necessary and desirable) for professional satisfaction and growth?

36. What information about yourself do you think you most like to hide even from yourself because it makes you uncomfortable to be aware of it?

37. What is your style of dealing with conflict? How would you improve your approach? To accomplish this, what is the next step you think you should take?

38. How much time alone do you need to remain balanced? What are the ways you see that such time is scheduled for yourself?

39. How do you know when you've lost your sense of perspective? What steps do you take to regain or maintain it?

40. What role does a sense of humor and laughter play in keeping you and the situation you are in from getting unnecessarily "heavy" or overwhelming?

41. What "little things" in life do you treasure and would miss if they were not present in your life? What are the big things? How do you show that you appreciate them?

42. What professional accomplishments are you very proud of? What are some future ones you'd very much like to achieve?

43. Describe how you organize your schedule and how much control you have in your life. Are there ways this might be improved?

44. When and with whom are you most apt to react in an angry way? In a cowardly way? By withdrawing? Through avoidance?

45. Would you and others at work and home best describe you as assertive, passive, passive-aggressive, or aggressive? Is there a difference between your style in your personal

and work/professional life? If so, how would you account for that?

46. What are the major areas of imbalance in your life? How are you addressing them? If you are not, what are some of the reasons you feel it is important to do so at this point in your life?

47. Do you know how to observe your feelings and behavior, then explore what cognitions (ways of thinking, perceiving, and understanding) and beliefs (schemata) are giving rise to them? If so, do you then dispute your dysfunctional thoughts as a way to keep perspective and avoid unnecessary stress/depressive thinking/self-condemnation? If not, how might you improve this area of self-awareness, self-monitoring, and increased recognition of the style of one's self-talk especially when under undue stress or after a failure?

48. What are the most unhealthy ways you are now meeting your needs or "medicating" yourself? What unhealthy gratifications are you concerned that you might avail yourself of in the future? What are you doing to prevent, limit, or avoid this from happening?

49. What is the overall design of your daily, weekly, monthly, and yearly breaks for leisure, relaxation, quiet, and recreation? How would you describe your feelings about these times (feeling guilt, deserving, feeling uncomfortable, preoccupied with work, blissful, resentful that they are too few and far between, etc.)?

50. What are the types of negative statements you normally make to yourself when you fail?

51. What are the healthiest ways you cope with life's difficulties? What are the most immature and unhealthy ways?

52. In what ways are you collaborative with other members at work? What are the benefits and struggles you experience with such collaboration?

53. What professional and personal resentments do you still carry and when are they most likely to surface?

54. Have you had any significant losses in the past several years? If so, what has your reaction been to them— initially, recently, now?

55. How do you view yourself in terms of physical aspects of your life (attractiveness, physical health, eating/drinking/ weight/smoking/medication and illegal drug use, and exercise patterns)?

56. What is your reaction to the statement, "Resilience is something you are born with"?

57. What are your feelings about asking for help in your personal life from your family? A colleague? Professional organization? Your physician? A psychiatrist, psychologist, or counselor? A clergyperson?

58. In your professional life or the work arena, when have you been tempted to step over personal, sexual, financial, or other appropriate boundaries you should have with your customers or colleagues?

59. Is there someone in your circle of friends who is both kind yet clear and direct with you so you would feel at ease to share anything while receiving honest guidance?

60. What situations or with what type of persons do you feel most emotionally vulnerable? In other words, when have you reacted by going to either the extreme of over-involvement and preoccupation or closing down emotionally?

© 2009 Robert J. Wicks
rwicks@loyola.edu

An Individual Reflection Guide

1. We often tell ourselves "lies" about our behavior and make excuses for it because we don't want to give up the secondary gain involved (not having to expend the energy to change or having to embrace what we might perceive to be unpleasant about ourselves). Until the "payoffs" we receive for the behavior are unmasked as too costly and unnecessary, even the most destructive and immature defensive behavior will remain to cause us stress.

2. "Realistic" and "helpful" are important words in this question because they try to help us get around the resistance to change that is present when we feel any steps to reduce stress are beyond us; therefore, we don't have to do anything.

3. This question seeks to push us a bit further in an effort to get us to be more assertive and creative in our planning and actions regarding the stress in life.

4. Too often we resist change by being global in our definitions of what's causing stress in our lives. This question seeks to get more specific causes out in the open so they can be addressed more directly either by ourselves or with our mentor/peer group.

5. This question allows us to make an inventory of our strengths as well as areas of vulnerability or growing edges. The longer and more detailed the two lists are the more useful the responses will be. Also, looking for patterns in the list can be helpful in terms of planning interventions or attitude/schedule changes.

6. The only memory that is a problem is the one intentionally forgotten or unconsciously repressed because it retains power without our being aware of it. This question gives an opportunity to be honest again regarding those past events that are still sapping energy from us now and unconsciously impacting our behaviors in the present.

7. One of the goals in phrasing the question again with the word "realistic" is to try to break the logjam that occurs when we feel overwhelmed and think nothing can be done. Perspective and attitude have tremendous power; whereas people who burn out often lose an awareness of this and feel that unless someone else changes my environment, little benefit can result.

8. Once we believe that "only a burned-out person/ professional really cares and works hard," the psychological cost is immense. Moving against this societal and professional myth is essential if one is to undertake a program of self-care.

9. This is an opportunity to divide the *people* who we felt were professionally competent and personally attractive from the dysfunctional *behavior* they may have also modeled.

10. As a follow-up to question #9 this one asks for more information on how we can carry on the good heritage of our role models and leave behind their parallel defensive sides so we can become healthier in how we carry out our work.

11. There are some fantasies we should act on and others that would be dangerous if we did. Knowing the difference *ahead of time* is essential so acting out or violating boundaries with colleagues, family members, or customers is never done with the rationalization after the fact that: "It just happened."

12. This raises the need to have a self-care protocol and causes us to think in a more focused manner about the helpful and destructive ways one deals with the pressures in one's personal and professional life.

13. This question is designed to have you face your own resistances and defenses with the same energy and intellectual stamina as you face other issues in life.

14. "Workaholism" is a pattern that seems to go unchecked in many professionals' lives; this question helps us to not gloss over the work style that everyone seems to acknowledge is present in us but we can't seem to fully grasp ourselves. People continue to endure an immense amount of unnecessary stress with either the response, "It's part of the territory of my work," or "That's just the way I am."

15. This allows us to take a step back and to acknowledge the human doubts and insecurities that all people have. This is important because much defensive or compensatory behavior is driven by such unexamined dynamics.

16. Distractions waste a tremendous amount of time. Mistakes are often attributed to a lack of attention. This question helps us to see how we might systemically avoid unnecessary distraction or understand the dynamics involved in what needlessly preoccupies us at times.

17. Making a list of how our personality both negatively and positively impacts certain types of individuals or all people when we are in certain moods equips us to better manage our style of dealing with the world. By having greater awareness in this area we can avoid so many potential relational problems that it is worth returning to this question to see what else we might add as illustrations of when and how we improved or made situations worse. It is very hard to do this because of the tendency either to project the blame onto others on the one hand or simply

blame ourselves. Clarity and a nonjudgmental approach to ourselves and our behavior are needed here.

18. Knowing your own stress points and when you are particularly vulnerable is essential. Even basic steps like knowing when to keep quiet until we understand why we are reacting so strongly and can regain more of our composure can make a major difference in the stress level of interactions with others.

19. In many cases we believe we know why we entered the field of employment we did. However, there were many overlapping mature and immature reasons that we probably haven't thought about. Having this information is very valuable so that we can appreciate how to let the mature reasons grow and the other ones atrophy or take their proper place rather than ascending to a level where we make decisions for the wrong reasons.

20. Revisiting motivations that inspired and challenged us is essential if we are to keep and deepen the roles we have assumed in the lives of others. This reflection is very important especially with the jaded views of many in the culture with respect to certain professions or jobs.

21. Many awkward subjects that are sensitive for us to discuss with others we don't even reflect on in the safety of our solitude. This question gives us permission and encouragement to take some time to look at our sensitive issues and to start asking ourselves what we can do about them.

22. Healthy narcissism is good. It encourages us to take credit for good work, to be happy that we are in key roles caring for others, and helps us recognize when we become defensive because our ego is getting in the way when it shouldn't.

23. This question reacquaints us with both the joy and pain of being in the job we are in. It is being asked to foster greater clarity about what we don't like and to see if we can change it in some way. Even if we make minor alterations in a number of small areas we can experience great summative relief. But more than that, by gaining clarity about what we like best, we can remember to enjoy and take strength from these areas.

24. This is a standard "taking stock" question which asks us what is going on that we didn't anticipate so that if we need to do something about it we can do it before we get too derailed personally and professionally.

25. Frustrations drain energy. By naming them we are taking the first step to understanding why they are so frustrating to us whereas others don't find them so. Once they can be understood in this way they will lose some of their power; then we can catch ourselves when we repeat this pattern so we don't continue it any longer than need be.

26. Thoughts of job change often come during times when we have an aggregate of negative elements in our work/ professional lives. By reviewing when and how we thought of moving or actually did move, we can learn from this

process in ways that prevent unnecessary moves or help us realize better when such a significant change is needed to relieve intractable stress or to open up new possibilities.

27. This question is important for all of us to ask so we can be honest with ourselves as to how we feel about the field and our role in it. It also pulls us into the future to give some sense of the tone of our outlook and begs the question, What would I need to do to make this more positive for myself?

28. Our self-care protocol is examined here. At the very least, this question will encourage us to see if we have a plan in place. If it is informal, then it will help us write down what we are actually doing and give us a sense of how we might improve it.

29. Knowing who is able to "push our emotional buttons" is an important antidote to unnecessary stress. This question allows us to gain greater clarity which is much needed if we are to remain psychologically healthy in tense situations. Otherwise, the only thing that will happen is we will project the blame on certain types of people or blame ourselves for the negative consequences that result.

30. Looking at the interchange between personal and professional well-being and how they impact each other helps us see that most adversity involves a more complex dynamic than we at first imagined it to have.

31. Breaking down fear into specifics allows us to discuss the particulars with mentors and colleagues whom we trust so

we can deal with the fears constructively rather than having them haunt us to no purpose. Just to name and discuss them can help alleviate stress.

32. Powerlessness is an element in all of us. However, once again, simply applying attention to such areas tends to diminish their quiet hold on us.

33. This is a chance to see what, if any, differences we feel about our profession/occupation and the stresses it holds as opposed to the stresses we observe in other fields. It allows us also to normalize some of our stress because we have much in common with many fields but don't often acknowledge this.

34. Methods to self-awareness such as reflection, meditation, journaling, receiving and giving supervision, personal daily debriefing, receiving mentoring, and formal/informal peer group discussions all can help us become better attuned to our styles. This question helps us visit this area to see if any or all of these approaches are present in some way, and if not, why not.

35. By breaking down needs, we can begin to see those cases where we are depriving ourselves of essential components of personal or professional well-being and where we have developed a series of induced needs that are psychologically costly.

36. This question again visits the issue of shame. It allows us to free up those areas we have partially hidden even from ourselves so we can finally learn more from them.

Once revealed, those hidden areas are reduced to their proportion rather than dominating our perspective.

37. Each person has a different style of dealing with conflict. It is not good or bad—it just is. By taking this approach and seeking to see the pros and cons of our style we can take steps to improve upon it. Most people focus on who is right or wrong rather than on the style of conflict resolution. That is why this question—if responded to in detail—can produce much fruit and be a significant factor in stress reduction for ourselves and those with whom we interact.

38. Time by ourselves is often considered a luxury. However, whether you are an introvert or an extrovert, time alone is essential for renewal, reflection, reassessment, and to break the movement of an often driven schedule. Having greater intention about where, how, and when to insert periods of solitude is necessary for one's mental health. For those who are religiously-minded it is an often advocated way of connecting to one's spiritual center.

39. Our loss of perspective is often more evident to others than to ourselves. However, there are signs that we have lost distance and a sense of proportion. They include: extreme emotion, withdrawal, an unnecessary increase in the pace of activity, or preoccupation. Once we know this we can then ask ourselves how to best regain perspective. It may be a short walk, a phone call to a friend, or just breathing slowly and remaining silent until we regain

more of our composure. This approach helps us realize that we can lose perspective and need to regain it in some way almost every day. It also prevents the three classic dangers that come about when perspective is lost: projection, self-blame, and discouragement. Being intrigued with the dynamics within us as well as within the context in which the loss of perspective occurred is naturally more healthy and productive. Answering this question fully helps support this good movement in our professional and personal lives.

40. Too often on the way to taking our work seriously, we take ourselves too seriously. This question highlights that reality for all of us and helps us remember to continually appreciate that laughter is good medicine and a sense of humor keeps things light.

41. Deep gratefulness is one of the major preventatives and antidotes to a loss of perspective. We have much to be grateful for—including our family, friends, and work. Gratefulness is not natural for most of us; whereas negative reactions seem to rise spontaneously and without effort. Self-training in this area starts with greater awareness that everything is a gift. This gratefulness is a powerful antidote to burnout. This is so because when you are feeling constantly nourished by your surroundings you retain a better sense of balance. Gratefulness increases our sensitivity to what events and people are giving us so we don't take them for granted, belittle them, or even miss them.

42. Taking stock of your accomplishments is an act of healthy narcissism. It also aids, once again, in prevention of the loss of perspective that comes when we just focus on our failures, absences, and struggles without seeing how far we have come. It also aids us in planning for the future, stirring up new hope in our hearts rather than having us just go through the motions every day.

43. Time management is often not taught in schools. Yet, one of the causes of stress is disorganization or distraction at work. This question raises the possibility that we have more under our control than we are willing to acknowledge. In developing a self-care protocol, we must address this area in some way so we can use management/organizational skills to lessen stress.

44. By picturing actual people in our lives that cause attack or flight reactions we can begin to better understand what it is that this type of person is triggering in our lives. This allows us to better understand and cope with what we fear or are concerned will happen. Once again, in most people's lives, the fact that certain people or personality types upset us is accepted as something that can't be changed. The luxury of avoidance must not be accepted because we will invariably come into contact with such people again.

45. Appreciating our style by honestly looking at ourselves should be easier at this point in the questionnaire since by now, we are hopefully into the exercise of looking with

a sense of intrigue, and not with self-condemnation or denial. As we do this it is important to begin to see the differences in our styles at work and at home and try to better understand that difference. It will help in improving our interaction skills both at home and at work.

46. Imbalances need not remain in our lives. They also need not be radically corrected overnight. Such a desire often ends up in our acting rashly rather than courageously to provide the necessary balance that will result in personal and professional well-being.

47. Picking up on our feelings about things and then examining any dysfunctional thoughts and beliefs that may underlie our feelings allows us to replace them with healthier ones. This is an important step in maintaining perspective and excellent mental health. This question also helps us to identify and raise the volume of our "self-talk" so we don't let negative thinking act as the invisible puppeteer in our psyche.

48. Workaholism, alcohol abuse, improper use of medication, sexual acting out, compulsive activity (eating, buying, or gambling/stock market speculation) are but a few of the ways we "medicate" ourselves. Knowing how, when, and to what extent we do this is an important first step in addressing this problematic area which is often a primary focus of our denial.

49. Time off during the day, week, month, and year are conscious decisions that effectively prevent and limit burnout.

This area, as well as our feelings about it, is important to address as part of self-care.

50. Failure is part and parcel of involvement. The more we are involved and the more delicate problems we must face at work, the more we will fail. That is a statistical reality because we can't be perfect. Case closed. Therefore, knowing how we deal with failure, since it is often a part of what we do, helps to diminish unnecessary anxiety and avoidable stress.

51. This question addresses overall style when we are faced with obstacles and asks for an inventory of our talents and defenses. As in some of the other questions, this seeks a review and also goes hand in hand with other questions to check the reliability of our previous responses.

52. Collaboration has often been seen as necessary but not realistic by many. Yet, if we are to be effective in our occupation or profession there needs to be a team effort in which each member of the team is respected, has input into the services we provide to others, and is given as much autonomy as is appropriate. Your understanding of and attitude toward collaboration is explored in this question as well.

53. Resentments are psychological powder kegs that lie in the preconscious and may break through when triggered by an event or person in our environment—especially when sleep deprivation or another problem or shortcoming makes us more vulnerable. By unearthing these resentments

we prevent them from remaining as hidden psychological cancers that can devour us from within.

54. Since dealing with the issues of death and dying are part of the territory in all people's lives, being aware of our own losses and how we have dealt with or avoided dealing with them, is quite helpful.

55. Taking note of our physical prowess and those elements that support it or are destructive to it is something that many of us paradoxically avoid. This question asks for a detailed response which is undertaken without blame but with honesty and a willingness to consider measured change that you can sustain without feeling overwhelmed or deprived.

56. No person can be perfect with all persons at work and home. How we answer this question provides some insight into our view of the expectations we have of ourselves.

57. We can never go it alone. Also, sometimes it is important to treat ourselves to a defined period of therapy or mentoring so we can work through failures, deepen our personal lives, and learn new creative ways of improving personal and professional well-being. This question looks at how we avail ourselves of help, collaboration, supervision, and support.

58. Honesty in this question allows us to notice the "emotional flags" that warn us when we might violate boundaries with our colleagues or those we serve at work. Everyone has a vulnerable place in their lives where

boundary violation is possible. Knowing ahead of time what these may be or what type of person we would be most vulnerable with is essential.

59. This asks us to define the question with whom do we feel both freedom and clarity. At the very least, asking it points to the tenet that if we don't have a person like this in our lives we run the risk of going off course in our professional and personal lives. It also points to the need to ensure that we have steady contact with someone like this, and if we don't, to find someone who can fit this role.

60. Becoming callous or overemotional is a constant danger in dealing with ongoing intense interpersonal situations. This question is designed to help us explore when and how this happens. As with the other questions, it is asking us not to take our reactions for granted but to explore them further so we can both understand ourselves better and plan for change that is productive in both personal and professional ways.

© 2009 Robert J. Wicks
rwicks@loyola.edu

RESILIENCE

Brem, M.L. (2001). *The seven greatest truths about successful women: How you can achieve financial independence, professional freedom, and personal joy.* New York: Perigee Books.

Brooks, R., & Goldstein, S. (2004). *The power of resilience: Achieving balance, confidence, and personal strength in your life.* New York: McGraw-Hill.

Crawford, R. (1998). *How high can you bounce? Turn setbacks into comebacks.* New York: Bantam Dell.

Domar, A. D., & Dreher, H. (2001). *Self-nurture: Learning to care for yourself as effectively as you care for everyone else.* New York: Penguin.

Flach, F. (2004). *Resilience: Discovering a new strength at times of stress.* (Revised Ed.). Long Island City, NY: Hatherleigh Press.

Grotberg, E. (2003). *Resilience for today: Gaining strength from adversity*. Westport, CT: Praeger Publishers.

Kottler, J. A. (2003). *On being a therapist*. San Francisco: John Wiley & Sons.

Leiter, M. P., & Maslach, C. (2005). *Banishing burnout: Six strategies for improving your relationship with work* (3rd ed.). San Francisco: Jossey-Bass.

Miller, B. (2005). *The woman's book of resilience: Twelve qualities to cultivate*. Boston, MA: Conari Press.

Nash, L. (2000). *The bounce back quotient: Fifty-two action oriented ideas for bouncing back from any change or setback in life*. St. Louis: Prism Publications.

Orsborn, C. (1997) *The art of resilience: One hundred paths to wisdom and strength in an uncertain world*. New York: Three Rivers Press.

Reinhold, B. B. (1997). *Toxic work: How to overcome stress, overload and burnout and revitalize your career*. New York: Plume.

Reivich, K., & Shatte, A. (2002). *The resilience factor: Seven keys to finding your inner strength and overcoming life's hurdles*. New York: Broadway Books.

Schnall, M. (2000). *What doesn't kill you makes you stronger: Turning bad breaks into blessings*. Cambridge, MA: De Capo Press.

Siebert, A. (1994). *The survivor personality: Why some people are stronger, smarter, and more skillful at handling life's difficulties . . . and how you can be too*. New York: Perigee Books.

Viscott, D. (1996). *Emotional resilience: Simple truths for dealing with the unfinished business of your past*. New York: Three River Press.

Walsh, F. (2006). *Strengthening family resilience* (2nd ed.). New York: Guilford Press.

Wolin, S. J. & Wolin, S. (1993). *The resilient self: How survivors of troubled families rise above adversity*. New York: Villard.

MINDFULNESS

Batchelor, S. (1997). *Buddhism without beliefs.* New York: Riverhead Books.

Beck, C. (1989). *Everyday zen: Love and work.* San Francisco: Harper San Francisco.

Brach, T. (2003). *Radical acceptance: Embracing your life with the heart of a Buddha.* New York: Bantam Dell.

Brantley, J. (2007). *Calming your anxious mind.* (2nd ed.). Oakland: New Harbinger Publications.

Brantley, J. (2003). *Calming your anxious mind.* Oakland: New Harbinger Publications.

Brazier, D. (1954/1995). *Zen therapy.* New York: John Wiley & Sons.

Chodron, P. (2001). *The wisdom of no escape and the path of loving-kindness.* Boston: Shambhala Publications.

Dalai Lama & Cutler, H. (1998). *The art of happiness: A handbook for living.* New York: Riverhead Books.

Epstein, M. (1995). *Thoughts without a thinker: Psychotherapy from a Buddhist perspective.* New York: Basic Books.

Germer, C., Siegel, R., & Fulton, P. (Eds.). (2005). *Mindfulness and psychotherapy.* New York: Guilford Press.

Goldstein, J. (1993). *Insight meditation: The practice of freedom.* Boston: Shambhala Publications.

Goldstein, J., & Kornfield, J. (1987). *Seeking the heart of wisdom.* Boston: Shambhala Publications.

Goldman, D. (2003). *Destructive emotions: How can we overcome them?* New York: Bantam Dell.

Gunaratana, B. (2002). *Mindfulness in plain English.* Somerville, MA: Wisdom Publications.

Hanh, T. N. (1987). *The miracle of mindfulness.* Boston: Beacon Press.

Hayes, S., Follette, V., & Linehan, M. (Eds.). (2004). *Mindfulness and acceptance: Expanding the cognitive-behavioral tradition.* New York: Guilford Press.

Kabat-Zinn, J. (1990). *Full catastrophe living.* New York: Delacorte Press.

Kabat-Zinn, J. (1994). *Wherever you go there you are: Mindfulness meditation in everyday life.* New York: Hyperion.

Kabat-Zinn, J. (2005). *Coming to our senses: Healing ourselves and the world through mindfulness.* New York: Hyperion.

Kabat-Zinn, J. (2005). *Guided mindfulness meditation.* Series 1-3 (Compact disc). Box 547, Lexington, MA: Stress reduction CDs and tapes.

Kabat-Zinn, M. & Kabat-Zinn, J. (1998). *Everyday blessings: The inner work of mindful parenting.* New York: Hyperion.

Kornfield, J. (1993). *A path with heart: A guide through the perils and promises of spiritual life.* New York: Bantam Dell.

Kornfield, J. (2000). *After the ecstasy, the laundry: How the heart grows wise on the spiritual path.* New York: Bantam Dell.

Langer, E. (1989). *Mindfulness.* Cambridge, MA: Da Capo Press.

Linehan, M. (2005). *This one moment: Skills for everyday mindfulness.* Seattle: Behavioral Tech.

Salzberg, S. (1995). *Loving kindness: The revolutionary art of happiness.* Boston: Shambhala Publications.

Stern, D. (2004). *The present moment in psychotherapy and everyday life.* New York: W. W. Norton.

Suzuki, S. (1973). *Zen mind, beginner's mind.* New York: John Weatherhill.

Weiss, A. (2004). *Beginning mindfulness: Learning the way of awareness.* Novato, CA: New World Library.

Wicks, R. (2003). *Riding the dragon.* Notre Dame, IN: Sorin Books.

Williams, M., Teasdale, J., Segal, Z., & Kabat-Zinn, J. (2007). *The mindful way through depression: Freeing yourself from chronic unhappiness.* New York: Guilford Press.

POSITIVE PSYCHOLOGY

Aspinwall, L. G., & Staudinger, U. M. (Eds.). (2003). *A psychology of human strengths: Fundamental questions and future directions for a positive psychology.* Washington, DC: American Psychological Association.

Baumeister, R. F. (2005). *The cultural animal: Human nature, meaning, and social life.* Oxford: Oxford University Press.

Csikszenthmihalyi, M. (1990). *Flow: The psychology of optimal experience.* New York: Harper Perennial.

Csikszenthmihalyi, M. (1998). *Finding flow: The psychology of engagement with everyday life.* New York: Basic Books.

Czikszenthmihalyi, M., & Csikszentmihalyi, I. S. (Eds.). (2006). *A life worth living: Contributions to positive psychology.* New York: Oxford University Press.

Emmons, R. A., & McCullough, M. E. (Eds.). (2004). *The psychology of gratitude.* Oxford: Oxford University Press.

Fowers, B. J. (2005). *Virtue and psychology: Pursuing excellence in ordinary practices.* Washington, DC: American Psychological Association.

Gilbert, D. (2006). *Stumbling on happiness.* New York: Alfred A. Knopf.

Haidt, J. (2006). *The happiness hypothesis: Finding modern truth in ancient wisdom.* New York: Basic Books.

James, W. (2002). *The varieties of religious experience: A study in human nature.* New York: Modern Library.

Keyes, C. L. M., & Haidt, J. (2002). *Flourishing: Positive psychology and the life well-lived.* Washington, DC: American Psychological Association.

Linley, P. A., & Joseph, A. (Eds.). (2004). *Positive psychology in practice.* Hoboken, NJ: John Wiley & Sons.

Maslow, A. H. (1999). (3rd ed.). *Toward a psychology of being.* New York: John Wiley & Sons.

Norem, J. K. (2001). *The positive power of negative thinking.* Cambridge, MA: Basic Books.

Pearsall, P. (2003). *The Beethoven factor: The new positive psychology of hardiness, happiness, healing, and hope.* Charlottesville, VA: Hampton Roads Publishing Co.

Peterson, C. (2006). *A primer in positive psychology.* New York: Oxford University Press.

Peterson, C., & Seligman, M. E. P. (Eds.). (2004). *Character strengths and virtues: A handbook and classification.* Oxford: American Psychological Association & Oxford University Press.

Seligman, M. E. P. (1998). *Learned optimism: How to change your mind and your life.* New York: Pocket Books.

Seligman, M. E. P. (1993). *What you can change . . . and what you can't: The complete guide to successful self-improvement.* New York: Ballantine Books.

Seligman, M. E. P. (2002). *Authentic happiness: Using the new positive psychology to realize your potential for lasting fulfillment.* New York: Free Press.

Snyder, C. R., & Lopez, S. J. (Eds.). (2002). *Handbook of positive psychology.* Oxford: Oxford University Press.

CONTEMPORARY BIOGRAPHIES/ AUTOBIOGRAPHIES OF RESILIENT PEOPLE

Angelou, M. (1981). *The heart of a woman.* New York: Random House.

Angelou, M. (1983). *I know why the caged bird sings.* New Providence, NJ: Bantam Dell.

Angelou, M. (1997). *Wouldn't take nothing for my journey now.* New Providence, NJ: Bantam Dell.

Armstrong, L. & Jenkins, S. (2000). *It's not about the bike: My journey back to life.* New York: Putnam.

Beamer, L. & Abraham, K. (2002). *Let's roll!: Ordinary people, extraordinary courage.* Carol Stream, IL: Tyndale House Publishers.

Ghandi, M. & Fischer, L. (1962). *The essential ghandi: An anthology of his writings on his life, work, and ideas.* New York: Vintage.

Dalai Lama. (1962, 1990). *My land and my people: The original autobiography of his holiness the Dalai Lama of Tibet.* New York: Warner Books.

Mandela, N. (1994, 1995). *Long walk to freedom: The autobiography of Nelson Mandela.* New York: Little, Brown and Company.

Allen, J. (2006). *Rabble-rouser for peace: The authorized biography of Desmond Tutu.* New York: Simon & Schuster.

WORKS CITED

(1989). "An interview with Thich Nhat Hanh, Vietnamese Zen Master," *Common boundary*, Nov./Dec., 16.

Auden, W. H. (1976). Introduction. In D. Hammarskjold (Ed.). *Markings* (p. ix). New York: Alfred A. Knopf.

Baker, E. (2003). *Caring for ourselves: A therapist's guide to personal and professional well-being.* Washington, DC: American Psychological Association.

Bloom, A. (1970). *Beginning to pray.* Ramsey, NJ: Paulist Press.

Bode, R. (1993). *First you have to row a little boat.* New York: Warner Books.

Brazier, D. (1954/1995). *Zen therapy.* New York: John Wiley & Sons.

Buber, M. (1966). *Way of man.* New York: Lyle Stuart.

Buckholz, E. (1997). *The call of solitude: Alonetime in a world of attachment.* New York: Simon & Schuster.

Buechner, C. Source unknown.

Burns, D. (1980). *Feeling good.* New York: New American Library.

Byrd, R. (1938/1995). *Alone.* New York: Kodansha.

Chadwick, D. (1999). *The crooked cucumber.* New York: Broadway Books.

Chekhov, A. Source unknown.

Chodron, P. (1997). *When things fall apart.* Boston: Shambala Publications.

Coster, J., & Schwebel, M. (1997). Well-functioning in professional psychologists. *Professional Psychology: Research and Practice, 28,* 10.

Courtois, C. A. (1999). *Recollections of sexual abuse: Treatment principles and guidelines.* New York: W. W. Norton & Co.

Cozolino, L. (2004). *The making of a therapist: A practical guide for the inner journey.* New York: W. W. Norton & Co.

Csikszentmihalyi, M. (2000). *Beyond boredom and anxiety.* San Francisco: Jossey-Bass. (Original work published in 1975).

Dalai Lama. (2000). *The path to tranquility.* New York: Penguin.

Day, D. Source unknown.

Domar, A., & Dreher, H. (2000). *Self-nurture: Learning to care for yourself as effectively as you care for everyone else.* New York: Penguin.

Dubois, D. (1983). Renewal of prayer. *Lumen Vitae, 38*(3), 273–274.

Edelwich, J., & Brodsky, A. (1980). *Burnout.* New York: Human Sciences Press.

Foy, D., Drescher, K., Fits, A., & Kennedy, K. (2003). Post-traumatic stress disorder. In R. Wicks, R. Parsons, & D. Capps (Eds.), *Clinical handbook of pastoral counseling Vol. 3* (pp. 274-277). Mahwah, NJ: Paulist Press.

Fredrickson, B. L. (1998). What good are positive emotions? *Review of General Psychology, 2,* 300–319.

Fredrickson, B. L. (2000). Cultivating positive emotions to optimize health and well-being. *Prevention and Treatment, 3.* Document available at http://journals.apa.org/prevention. Accessed February 8, 2005.

Fredrickson, B. L. (2001). The role of positive emotions in positive psychology: The broaden-and-build theory of positive emotions. *American Psychologist, 56,* 218—226.

Fredrickson, B. L. (2004). The broaden-and-build theory of positive emotions. *Philosophical Transactions of the Royal Society of London (Biological Sciences), 359,* 1367–1377.

Germer, C. K., Siegel, R. D., & Fulton, P. R. (Eds.). (2005). *Mindfulness and psychotherapy.* New York: Guilford Press.

Gill, J. (1980). Burnout: A growing threat in ministry. *Human Development, 1,* 24–25.

Gorky, M. (1996). *Gorky: My childhood.* London: Penguin.

Gunaratana, B. (2002). *Mindfulness in plain English.* Somerville, MA: Wisdom Publications.

Hay, G. (1967). *The way to happiness.* New York: Simon & Schuster.

Herman, J. (1997). *Trauma and recovery: The aftermath of violence—from domestic abuse to political terror.* New York: Basic Books.

Kabat-Zinn, J. (1994). *Wherever you go there you are: Mindfulness meditation in everyday life.* New York: Hyperion.

Kaplan, A. (1982). *Meditation and kabbalah.* York Beach, ME: Samuel Weiser.

Keller, P. A., & Ritt, L. (Eds.). (1984). *Innovations in clinical practice: A sourcebook Vol. 3.* Sarasota, FL: Professional Resource Exchange.

Kornfield, J. (1993). *A path with heart: A guide through the perils and promises of spiritual life.* New York: Bantam Dell.

Kornfield, J. (2000). *After the ecstasy, the laundry: How the heart grows wise on the spiritual path.* New York: Bantam Dell.

Kottler, J. (1989). *On being a therapist.* San Francisco: Jossey-Bass.

Kottler, J. A., & Hazler, R. J. (1997). *What you never learned in graduate school: A survival guide for therapists.* New York: W. W. Norton & Co.

Leech, K. (1980). *True prayer.* San Francisco: Harper & Row.

Linehan, M. (1993). *Cognitive-behavioral treatment of borderline personality disorder.* New York: Guilford Press.

Linehan, M. (2005). This one moment: Skills for everyday mindfulness. DVD.

Lynn, K. S. (1987). Ernest Hemingway: A psychological autopsy of a suicide. *Psychiatry: Interpersonal & Biological Processes, 69,* 351–361.

Maddi, S. R., & Khoshaba, D. M. (2005). *Resilience at work: How to succeed no matter what life throws at you.* New York: American Management Association.

Maslach, C., & Jackson, S. E. (1981). The measurement of experienced burnout. *Journal of Occupational Behavior, 2,* 99–113.

McCaffrey , R., & Fairbank, J. (1985). Behavioral assessment and treatment of accident-related posttraumatic stress disorder: Two case studies. *Behavior Therapy, 16,* 406–416.

McCuhan, M. Source unknown.

Meade, M. Source unknown.

Merton, T. (1988). *A vow of conversation.* New York: Farrar, Straus, and Giroux.

Morgan, S. (2005). *Depression: Turning toward life.* In C. K. Germer, R. D. Siegel, & P. R. Fulton (Eds.). (2005). *Mindfulness and psychotherapy* (pp. 130–151). New York: Guilford Press.

Nouwen, H. (1981). *Making all things new.* New York: Harper & Row.

Parsons, R. D., & Wicks, R. J. (Eds.). (1983). *Passive-aggressiveness: Theory and practice.* New York: Brunner/Mazel Publishers, Inc.

Peterson, C. (2006). *A primer in positive psychology.* New York: Oxford University Press.

Pfifferling, J. H. (1986). Cultural antecedents promoting professional impairment. In C. D. Scott & J. Hawk (Eds.). *Heal thyself: The health of health care professionals* (pp. 3–18). New York: Brunner/Mazel Publishers, Inc.

Pope, K. S., & Vasquez, M. J. T. (2005). *How to survive and thrive as a therapist.* Washington, DC: American Psychological Association.

Reinhold, B. B. (1997). *Toxic work: How to overcome stress, overload and burnout and revitalize your career.* New York: Plume.

Reivich, K., & Shatte, A. (2002). *The resilience factor: Seven keys to finding your inner strength and overcoming life's hurdles.* New York: Broadway Books.

Rilke, R. M. (1954/2004). *Letters to a young poet* (Revised ed.). New York: W. W. Norton & Company.

Riegle, R. (2003). *Dorothy Day: Portraits by those who knew her.* Maryknoll, NY: Orbis.

Rinpoche, S. (1992). *The Tibetan book of living and dying.* New York: Harper Collins.

Rodman, R. (1985). *Keeping hope alive.* New York: Harper & Row.

Sanders, L. (1982). *The case of Lucy Bending.* New York: Putnam.

Schmuck, P., & Sheldon, K. M. (2001). Introduction. In P. Schmuck & K. M. Sheldon (Eds.). *Life goals and well-being: Towards a positive psychology of human striving.* Cambridge, MA: Hogrefe & Huber Publishing.

Scott, C., & Hawk, J. (Eds.). (1986). *Health thyself: the health of health care professionals.* New York: Brunner/Mazel Publishers, Inc.

Seligman, M. E. P. (2002). *Authentic happiness: Using the new positive psychology to realize your potential for lasting fulfillment.* New York: Free Press.

Seaward, B. (2000). *Managing stress in emergency medical services.* Sudbury, MA: American Academy of Orthopaedic Surgeons/Jones and Bartlett.

Skovolt, T. M. (2001). *The resilient practitioner: Burnout prevention and self-care strategies for counselors, therapists, teachers, and health professionals.* Boston: Allyn & Bacon.

Storr, A. (1988). *On solitude.* New York: Bantam Dell.

Strand, C. (1988). *The wooden bowl.* New York: Hyperion.

Sussman, M. B. (1992). *A curious calling: Unconscious motivations for practicing psychotherapy.* Northvale, NJ: Jason Aronson.

Warner, C. (1992). *The last word: A treasury of women's quotes.* Englewood Cliffs, NJ: Prentice Hall Trade.

Weiss, A. (2004). *Beginning mindfulness: Learning the way of awareness.* Novato, CA: New World Library.

Wicks, R. (1986). *Availability.* New York: Crossroad.

Wicks, R. (1988). *Living simply in an anxious world.* Mahwah, NJ: Paulist Press.

Wicks, R. (1992). *Touching the holy.* Notre Dame, IN: Ave Maria Press.

Wicks, R. (1995). The stress of spiritual ministry: Practical suggestions on avoiding unnecessary distress. In R. Wicks (Ed.), *Handbook of spirituality for ministers, Vol. 1.* Mahwah, NJ: Paulist Press.

Wicks, R. (1997). *After fifty: Spiritually embracing your own wisdom years.* New York: Paulist Press.

Wicks, R. (1998). *Living a gentle, passionate life.* Mahwah, NJ: Paulist Press.

Wicks, R. (2000). *Simple changes.* Notre Dame, IN: Thomas More/Sorin Books.

Wicks, R. (2002). *Riding the dragon.* Notre Dame, IN: Sorin Books.

Wicks, R. (2003). Countertransference and burnout in pastoral counseling. In R. Wicks, R. Parsons, & D. Capps (Eds.), *Clinical handbook of pastoral counseling, Vol. 3* (p. 336). Mahwah, NJ: Paulist Press.

Wicks, R. (2006). *Overcoming secondary stress in medical and nursing practice: A guide to professional resilience and personal well-being.* New York: Oxford University Press.

Wicks, R. (2008) *The resilient clinician.* New York: Oxford University Press.

Wicks, R., & Hamma, R. (1996). *Circle of friends: Encountering the caring voices in your life.* Notre Dame, IN: Ave Maria Press.

Williams, E., Konrad, T., Scheckler, W., Pathman, D., Linzer, M., McMurray , J., et al. (2001). Understanding physicians' intentions to withdraw from practice: The role of job satisfaction, job stress, and mental and physical health. *Health Care Management Review,* 26(1), 15.

Zaslove, M. (2001). American Academy of Family Physicians. *Curbside consultation: A case of physician burnout.* American Family Physician. http://www.aafp.org/afp/20010801/curbside.html

I am grateful for the following permissions to use previously copyrighted material:

INDEX